CONTENTS

SOCIAL SECURITY'S IMPROVED DISABILITY DETERMINATION PROCESS

THURSDAY, JUNE 15, 2006

U.S. HOUSE OF REPRESENTATIVES,
COMMITTEE ON WAYS AND MEANS,
SUBCOMMITTEE ON SOCIAL SECURITY,
Washington, DC.

The Subcommittee met, pursuant to notice, at 11:04 a.m., in room B–318, Rayburn House Office Building, Hon. Jim McCrery (Chairman of the Subcommittee) presiding.

[The advisory announcing the hearing follows:]

ADVISORY

FROM THE COMMITTEE ON WAYS AND MEANS

SUBCOMMITTEE ON SOCIAL SECURITY

FOR IMMEDIATE RELEASE
June 07, 2006
No. SS–16

CONTACT: (202) 225–9263

McCrery Announces Hearing on Social Security's Improved Disability Determination Process

Congressman Jim McCrery, (R–LA), Chairman, Subcommittee on Social Security of the Committee on Ways and Means, today announced that the Subcommittee will hold a hearing on the Social Security Administration (SSA)'s improved disability determination process. **The hearing will take place on Thursday, June 15, 2006, in room B–318 Rayburn House Office Building, beginning at 11:00 a.m.**

In view of the limited time available to hear witnesses, oral testimony at this hearing will be from invited witnesses only. However, any individual or organization not scheduled for an oral appearance may submit a written statement for consideration by the Committee and for inclusion in the printed record of the hearing.

BACKGROUND:

The SSA administers two Federal disability programs: Disability Insurance (DI), and Supplemental Security Income (SSI). The DI program provides benefits to disabled workers and their families based on previous employment covered by Social Security, and is funded primarily with Social Security payroll taxes. The SSI program is a means-tested income assistance program funded with general revenues.

Workloads from these two programs have placed increasing demands on the agency. The DI and SSI applications to Federally-funded State Disability Determination Service agencies for a decision have increased 22 percent over the past five years, from 2.1 million in Fiscal Year (FY) 2000 to 2.55 million in FY 2005. Despite the increased workloads, the SSA has increased its productivity by 12.6 percent since 2001. However, the rapid rise in applications, coupled with budgetary constraints, have resulted in longer processing times for cases heard by Administrative Law Judges—from 415 days in FY 2005 to 477 days in April 2006. The number of hearing requests waiting for a decision has increased from about 708,000 in FY 2005 to 727,629 in April 2006, and the Agency expects this number to rise to 767,000 in FY 2007.

The Commissioner of Social Security, Jo Anne B. Barnhart, undertook a comprehensive initiative to evaluate and implement substantive process reforms to the disability determination process. These process improvements are built upon the SSA's new electronic disability folder system, which is being implemented on a phased-in basis. As the Commissioner has stated in previous testimony, her goal for the reforms has been to have the right decision made as early as possible in the process.

The Subcommittee has closely monitored the progress of this initiative since the Commissioner announced her intent to move forward at a Subcommittee hearing in September 2003. After extensive consultation with key stakeholders, including two Subcommittee hearings, the SSA published its final rule on March 31, 2006. The final rule will be phased in beginning August 1, 2006. In sum, the Disability Service Improvement rule (DSI) requires quick decisions (in 20 days or less) for individuals with clear-cut disabilities; improves medical and vocational expert access and qualifications; and creates a new position, the Federal Reviewing Official, to review State agency determinations upon the request of the claimant. The reconsideration step of the current appeals process is eliminated. The DSI also implements a new quality assurance process at every decision-making level. A description of the key components of the final rule may be found on the SSA's website at: *http://www.ssa.gov/disability-new-approach/*.

In announcing the hearing, Chairman McCrery stated, "I commend the Commissioner of Social Security and the dedicated employees of the Agency for initiating service improvements to the disability determination process. Now the hard work of implementation begins. I look forward to learning how the public's comments were incorporated into the final regulation and hearing how best to transform the regulation into action."

FOCUS OF THE HEARING:

The Subcommittee will examine the SSA's final regulation, including how the Agency addressed public comments in developing its final rule and how implementation will proceed.

DETAILS FOR SUBMISSION OF WRITTEN COMMENTS:

Please Note: Any person(s) and/or organization(s) wishing to submit for the hearing record must follow the appropriate link on the hearing page of the Committee website and complete the informational forms. From the Committee homepage, *http://waysandmeans.house.gov*, select *"109th Congress"* from the menu entitled, *"Hearing Archives"* (*http://waysandmeans.house.gov/Hearings.asp?congress=17*). Select the hearing for which you would like to submit, and click on the link entitled, *"Click here to provide a submission for the record."* Once you have followed the online instructions, completing all informational forms and clicking "submit" on the final page, an email will be sent to the address which you supply confirming your interest in providing a submission for the record. You ***MUST REPLY*** to the email and ***ATTACH*** your submission as a Word or WordPerfect document, in compliance with the formatting requirements listed below, by close of business Thursday, June 29, 2006. **Finally**, please note that due to the change in House mail policy, the U.S. Capitol Police will refuse sealed-package deliveries to all House Office Buildings. For questions, or if you encounter technical problems, please call (202) 225–1721.

FORMATTING REQUIREMENTS:

The Committee relies on electronic submissions for printing the official hearing record. As always, submissions will be included in the record according to the discretion of the Committee. The Committee will not alter the content of your submission, but we reserve the right to format it according to our guidelines. Any submission provided to the Committee by a witness, any supplementary materials submitted for the printed record, and any written comments in response to a request for written comments must conform to the guidelines listed below. Any submission or supplementary item not in compliance with these guidelines will not be printed, but will be maintained in the Committee files for review and use by the Committee.

1. All submissions and supplementary materials must be provided in Word or WordPerfect format and MUST NOT exceed a total of 10 pages, including attachments. Witnesses and submitters are advised that the Committee relies on electronic submissions for printing the official hearing record.

2. Copies of whole documents submitted as exhibit material will not be accepted for printing. Instead, exhibit material should be referenced and quoted or paraphrased. All exhibit material not meeting these specifications will be maintained in the Committee files for review and use by the Committee.

3. All submissions must include a list of all clients, persons, and/or organizations on whose behalf the witness appears. A supplemental sheet must accompany each submission listing the name, company, address, telephone and fax numbers of each witness.

Note: All Committee advisories and news releases are available on the World Wide Web at *http://waysandmeans.house.gov*.

The Committee seeks to make its facilities accessible to persons with disabilities. If you are in need of special accommodations, please call 202–225–1721 or 202–226–3411 TTD/TTY in advance of the event (four business days notice is requested). Questions with regard to special accommodation needs in general (including availability of Committee materials in alternative formats) may be directed to the Committee as noted above.

Chairman MCCRERY. The hearing will come to order. Good morning.

Welcome, everyone, to our hearing on the Social Security Administration's (SSA) improved disability determination process.

We last focused on these issues at a joint hearing in September where Members of both this Subcommittee along with the Human Resources Subcommittee provided their feedback to the Commissioner regarding the proposed rule to improve the disability determination and appeals process.

Members from both sides of the aisle praised the Commissioner and the employees of the SSA for their continued, focused, and collaborative efforts to improve service delivery to those with disabilities.

Concerns were also raised, though, that the proposed changes to the system could make what is currently a non-adversarial administrative process into one that is more legalistic and burdensome for very vulnerable claimants.

In March of this year, another milestone was achieved when the final rule was published, but perhaps the most important milestone is just a few weeks away, when the Agency begins implementing the rule on August 1st in the Boston region. Then we will start determining whether the changes achieve the desired effect, enabling the right decision to be made as early as possible in the process.

As implementation moves forward, we all know the stakes are high, as disability benefits provide a crucial safety net for those most in need.

Commissioner Barnhart has said she is committed to making sure that the implementation proceeds carefully so that all claims are handled fairly and responsibly.

Today, we will learn how the Commissioner and her staff plan to carry out that commitment.

Following the Commissioner, our second panel will provide their views on the implementation and what we and the Commissioner need to be mindful of as the reforms proceed and expand beyond the Boston region.

Mr. Levin, would you like to make an opening statement?

Mr. LEVIN. Thank you very much, and I'm really very, very glad we're having this hearing.

You mentioned the importance of this matter for our society, the importance of this program for the disabled. This affects all of us.

I'm glad that we're having the Commissioner here and a broad range of people and viewpoints on the panel. I don't think we have anything to fear from a diversity of points of view.

In fact, I think we have a lot to gain from it, and hopefully it will all meld into an improved program, Disability Service Improvement (DSI).

Obviously, no regulation can spell out all the details and anticipate every circumstance, no matter how well they're put together, and the implementation obviously can make or break an initiative like this one.

I think there was widespread feeling about the importance of improving the disability process. I think we would all agree.

When we look back at the work of our offices, many, many times our offices, especially at home, were contacted because of issues relating to disability, and we know that changes were necessary. We also thought that some aspects of the proposed regulation had some real potential, but there were concerns of others.

So, people got their heads together, and not always together, but in the same room, to talk about this, and we appreciate the effort of you, the Commissioner, and everybody who is here today.

We also appreciate the important role that SSA employees and beneficiary representatives have played in helping to understand this regulation and the challenges ahead, and if I might just add briefly, I think that we very much agree that we need in the Congress to do our part to make sure there's adequate funding, because no matter how well a regulation is put together or its implementation is brought about, there's going to have to be adequate funding.

We're going today to go into the details of the regulation. One last word. An essential part of implementation is careful monitoring, and I understand, Commissioner, that you're going to track the results to assure that disability claimants are not harmed, but indeed their needs are looked after, and that there are no unintended results occurring from this and that the changes are going to have the desired effect. I'm sure that you are going to have—continue to have—excellent oversight that you have made sure happens.

We look forward to your testimony, and then the testimony of seven or eight—six or seven—people who are going to join us.

Chairman MCCRERY. Thank you, Mr. Levin.

Any other Members wishing to make an opening statement may present those in writing and they'll be included in the record.

We do have a rather full second panel, so let's proceed with Commissioner Barnhart. Welcome once again, and thank you again for the work you've done on this subject and for listening to our concerns throughout the rulemaking process.

You may summarize your remarks in about 5 minutes, and then if you would, take our questions.

You may proceed.

STATEMENT OF THE HONORABLE JO ANNE B. BARNHART, COMMISSIONER OF SOCIAL SECURITY, SOCIAL SECURITY ADMINISTRATION

Ms. BARNHART. Thank you, Mr. Chairman, Mr. Levin, and Members of the Subcommittee.

I'm always pleased to appear before you, but today I'm especially happy to be here, because I'm here to report that after 3 years of incredible effort and cooperation, our new disability determination process is a reality.

For the first time in 50 years, we're making significant changes to the SSA's disability determination process, changes that substantially increase our ability to make accurate decisions in a timely way, and that means better service to the American people.

My written statement outlines the elements of the new process and goes into it in a great bit of detail, but in the interests of time, I'm going to concentrate on how we got to this point.

As you know, it has been a long journey, and this Subcommittee has played an important role in this achievement. So, have many others within and outside SSA, and I want to thank you and everyone who participated, many of them here in this room, from the bottom of my heart.

I'm sure you know that there were people who told us that it would be impossible to make major comprehensive changes to the disability determination process, but we have done it, and we have succeeded because groups involved at every step in the disability process came together in a spirit of cooperation and professionalism.

Throughout this process, there was no finer example of that spirit than Eileen Sweeney. Sadly, Eileen passed away just a few days ago.

As this Committee well knows, Eileen was a tireless and talented advocate for America's most vulnerable, and we will all miss her insight, her expertise, and most of all, her humanity.

When I announced my new approach, I began a massive outreach effort to obtain and give thoughtful consideration to all comments on the current disability system and on our proposed improvements. I've acted upon my commitment to listen to you, to the interested parties and groups in both the government and the private sectors, and to the claimants and beneficiaries who rely on us to provide the best possible service.

During the official comment period on the Notice of Proposed Rulemaking (NPRM) alone, we received almost 900 comments, 883 to be precise. At the hearing last September on the proposed rule, Members of this Committee urged me to carefully consider the issues that were raised and the comments.

I want you to know, Mr. Chairman, that I personally read many of the comments in full myself, and I worked with my senior staff to review and discuss all of the comments.

We listened and we made changes in response. As a result, I believe the disability determination process that we will be implementing in our Boston Region on August 1st is both different and better than the original blueprint that I discussed with you on July 24, 2003, and the process that was outlined in the NPRM last July.

We were aware that many commenters perceived our proposed rule as favoring administrative efficiency over fairness, especially with regard to timeframes for submitting evidence before a hearing. When I testified last fall, this Subcommittee articulated those same concerns, as the Chairman pointed out.

I want to assure you that that was not our intent. I trust that was made clear by the substantive changes that we made in the final regulation.

Specifically, we addressed the concerns about giving claimants sufficient time to submit evidence in three ways.

First, we give claimants at least 75 days notice before a hearing instead of the 45 days provided for in the NPRM.

Second, the final rule allows claimants to submit evidence up to five business days before the hearing instead of the 20 days in the proposed rule.

Finally, we expanded the range of circumstances in which an administrative law judge (ALJ) will accept evidence that does not meet the five-day deadline.

Mr. Chairman, as I look back over the long road to the changes that we will begin implementing in just a few weeks, and I reflect on the spirit of cooperation, professionalism, and dedication to serving the public that has really permeated this entire process and been demonstrated by the men and women of Social Security, our Disability Determination Service (DDS) agencies, advocacy groups, and Members of Congress, I'm absolutely convinced we can make this happen. I am also convinced that the American public will benefit greatly.

I assure you that we will continue the dialog that has served this process so well, because this is not just about getting it done, it's about getting it done right.

You have my assurance that we're doing all that we can to make sure that we implement in an orderly and timely manner. In typical fashion, the hardworking men and women of SSA and our DDSs have pulled together and they're doing everything that must be done for us to move forward.

In closing, I want to publicly thank you again for your advice, insight, and support that have meant a great deal to the Agency and to me personally. I know that we can count on your continued support and advice as we make DSI a reality.

Thank you, Mr. Chairman. I'll be happy to try and answer any questions that the Members might have.

[The prepared statement of Ms. Barnhart follows:]

Statement of The Honorable Jo Anne B. Barnhart, Commissioner, Social Security Administration

Mr. Chairman, Mr. Levin, and Members of the Subcommittee,

I am always delighted to appear before you, but today I am especially pleased to be here. Today, I am here to report that, after three years of incredible effort and cooperation, our new disability determination process is a reality. For the first time in 50 years, we are making significant changes to the Social Security Administration's (SSA) disability determination process—changes that substantially increase our ability to make accurate disability decisions in a timely way. And that means better service to the American public.

I will outline the elements in the new process in a few moments, but first I want to take this opportunity to talk about how we got to this point. It has been a long journey, and the members of this subcommittee have shared with me the journey toward this achievement. And so have many others within and outside SSA. And I want to thank you and everyone who participated from the bottom of my heart.

When I became Commissioner in 2001, I said that I did not take this job to manage the status quo, and nowhere was the need for change more clear than in the disability process. I'm sure you know that there were people who told us that it would be impossible to make major, comprehensive changes to the disability determination process. But we have, and we have succeeded because groups involved at every step in the disability process came together in a spirit of cooperation and professionalism. We succeeded because of that spirit of cooperation, openness, and constructive dialogue that I have seen in the conversations we've had with people involved at every stage of the process.

As you know, when I announced my new approach, I began a massive outreach effort to obtain and give thoughtful consideration to all comments on the current disability system and on our proposed improvements. I have acted upon my commitment to listen to you, to the interested parties and groups in both the government and private sector, and to the claimants and beneficiaries who rely on us to provide the best possible service.

I personally participated in more than 100 meetings with more than 60 groups involved in the disability process—inside and outside of SSA. My staff conducted even more meetings and we received more than 1000 comments and recommendations over the Internet alone. I was very impressed with the spirit of cooperation and professionalism that these groups brought to our discussion.

When we published the proposed rule, I did not expect agreement on every element of the approach outlined in the NPRM. However, I hoped for—and got—a continuation of the same spirit that we saw in the initial outreach period.

During the comment period, SSA received almost 900 comments. At the hearing last September on the NPRM, members of this Subcommittee urged me to consider carefully the issues that were being raised in the comments. I want you to know that I personally read many of these comments in full and worked with my senior staff to review and discuss all of them.

We listened and made changes in response. The disability determination process that we will begin implementing in our Boston Region on August 1 is both different and better than the original blueprint I first discussed with you on July 24, 2003, and the process outlined in the Notice of Proposed Rulemaking we published in July 2005.

In drafting the final rule, we were aware that many commenters perceived our proposed rule as favoring administrative efficiency over fairness—especially in regard to timeframes for submitting evidence before a hearing. When I testified before this Subcommittee last fall, members of the Subcommittee articulated these same concerns. Let me assure you that was *not* our intent. The new approach spelled out in the final rule contains many changes which underscore my commitment to an open, inclusive dialogue in the true meaning of the word dialogue—which includes listening.

We addressed the concerns about giving claimants sufficient time to submit evidence in three ways. First, we will give claimants at least 75 days notice before a hearing instead of the 45 days proposed in the NPRM. This will allow claimants and their representatives enough time to gather all necessary evidence and prepare for the hearing. Second, the final rule allows claimants to submit evidence up to 5 business days before their hearing instead of 20. This gives the claimant more time to submit evidence and will ensure that all parties to the hearing have enough time before the hearing to review the evidence and prepare for the hearing. Third, we expanded the range of circumstances in which an ALJ will accept evidence that does not meet the 5-day deadline.

Final Rule

The final rule was published in the *Federal Register* on March 31. It explains the new procedures for adjudicating initial claims for disability insurance and for Supplemental Security Income based on disability or blindness. The preamble to the final rule explains in detail the changes from the NPRM that were made as a result of the comments the Agency received. We created a dedicated website, www.socialsecurity.gov/disability-new-approach, to provide you with information about the new regulation and background related to its development.

The new disability determination process takes full advantage of Social Security's new electronic disability claims system, or eDib. Using eDib technology, the DSI changes will shorten decision times and pay benefits to people who are clearly disabled much earlier. eDib also allows us to access the electronic folder from any location making possible many of the changes in the new process.

Changes to the NPRM

As I mentioned at the beginning of my statement, in drafting the final rule, we were aware that, although there was broad agreement on the need for change, numerous groups perceived our proposed rule as favoring administrative efficiency over fairness.

We made a number of changes in the final rule in addition to the changes in the timeframes for submitting evidence that I discussed a moment ago.

We added language to the final rule to make it clear that a claimant, unable to make a timely request within 60 days of receiving his or her initial notice, can request additional time to request a review both before and after the 60-day period has ended. The claimant will also be permitted to submit new evidence after requesting review up until the date of the Federal Reviewing official, or FedRO decision (I will discuss this provision in more detail later).

We heard many concerns with the proposal that the Decision Review Board, or DRB, would consider only statements that it requested from claimants. In response, in the final rule, we allow claimants to submit statements to the DRB whenever the DRB notifies a claimant that it will review his or her claim.

Without question, elimination of the Appeals Council and its effect on the Federal courts was the area in which the most concern has been raised. At present, all social security disability cases appealed to the Federal courts must first be reviewed by the Appeals Council. Despite this final administrative review, nearly 60% of all appealed cases are remanded to the Agency either "voluntarily" through requests made by our General Counsel or as a result of findings made by the courts. Accordingly, in the NPRM we proposed gradually to phase out the Appeals Council and replace it with a new DRB. While claimants would no longer have a right to request review of an ALJ decision, the DRB would review an equal number of error-prone allowances and denials.

Throughout the comment period, concerns were expressed about this approach by organizations representing disability claimants who expressed fears that clearly erroneous denial decisions might escape review. The Judicial Conference and others also expressed concern that the Federal courts might be inundated with meritorious claims that would otherwise have been intercepted and resolved by the Appeals Council. In both instances, these concerns centered on the question of whether the Agency could develop an effective method for selecting the cases to be reviewed by the DRB.

In response to these concerns, we have decided that the DRB will initially review *all* of the administrative law judge decisions—allowances and denials—issued in the Boston region. This 100 percent review will allow us carefully to design, test, and validate a predictive model for selecting a subset of all ALJ decisions for DRB review that include those most likely to be remanded by the U.S. District Courts. During this same period, we will analyze the effects of the new approach on the workload of the Federal courts within the region.

We also heard many concerns about the changes we proposed regarding our reopening rules. Many argued that our existing reopening rules already worked well for claims decided at the earlier stages of the process. In response, we decided that our existing reopening rules would continue to operate for all claims adjudicated prior to the hearing level. We retained other changes to the reopening rules to allow for the reopening of claims decided at the hearing level or beyond while at the same time ensuring that we could efficiently close the record, with good cause exceptions, after we have issued a final decision.

Overall, our expectation is that the disability service changes will result in substantial improvements that will enable claimants to receive more accurate, consistent, timely, and understandable decisions. We also believe that this rule ensures an adjudicatory process that is consistent with due process, will give claimants a meaningful opportunity to be heard, and make accurate allowances as early in the process as possible.

Changes in SSA's Structure

To improve the management of our initiative as we move forward, I made two major organizational changes at SSA. I created a new Deputy Commissioner-level office named the Office of Disability Adjudication and Review to manage the agency's disability adjudication process. The Office of Disability Adjudication and Review, or ODAR, will manage the new FedRO level, the hearings and appeal functions formerly managed by the Office of Hearings and Appeals, and the new Decision Review Board. I believe it is important to have a single Deputy Commissioner that I can rely on to manage effectively every level of our disability adjudication appeals process, so that I can be sure that the entire adjudicatory process is functioning efficiently and fairly for every single claimant.

I also established a new Office of Quality Performance to manage the Agency's newly developed and still evolving integrated quality system which I believe will improve our disability determination process, as well as other program areas such as the Social Security retirement program and the SSI age-based program. The new Office of Quality Performance will manage a new quality system that includes both in-line and end-of-line quality review throughout the new DSI process. The Office of Quality Performance will be able quickly to identify problem areas, implement corrective actions, and identify related training as we implement the new DSI process.

Features of the New System

So how does the new process work? In summary:

- The State Disability Determination Services (DDS) will continue to make the initial determination.

- Individuals who are clearly disabled will have a process through which favorable determinations can be made within 20 calendar days after the date the DDS receives the claim.
- A Medical and Vocational Expert System (MVES) will enhance the quality and availability of the medical and vocational expertise that our adjudicators at all levels need to make timely and accurate decisions.
- A new position at the Federal level—the Federal Reviewing Official, or FedRO—will be established to review state agency determinations upon the request of the claimant. We intend to have well-trained attorneys serve as FedROs and we expect that this level of review will help ensure more accurate and consistent decision making earlier in the process.
- The right of claimants to request and be provided a de novo hearing conducted by an administrative law judge is preserved.
- The record will be closed after the administrative law judge issues a decision, with provisions for good cause exceptions.
- A new body, the Decision Review Board (DRB), will be created to identify and correct decisional errors and to identify issues that may impede consistent adjudication at all levels of the process.
- And the Appeals Council will be gradually phased out as the new process is implemented throughout the nation.

Two key improvements are embedded in the process. First are improvements in documenting the record at each step, so that all relevant information is available to adjudicators, and the claimant fully understands the basis for whatever decision is made. Second is a greatly strengthened in-line and end-of-line quality review process. In addition, quality feedback loops at every level will foster continuous improvement.

Implementation

The DSI process will be rolled out in a careful and measured manner. This gradual implementation will allow us to monitor the effects that the changes are having in each region, on our entire disability process, and the Federal courts. The lessons that we learn in the early stages of implementation will help us as we move into the later stages of the roll-out.

Just as we did with the implementation of our electronic system, implementation will be phased in and if we find that additional improvements are needed during the roll-out, we can and will make them. We will continue to listen to those with concerns, and we will make changes when necessary.

Moreover as we roll out the DSI process we intend to continue and expand our efforts to make sure that all adjudicators make their determinations and decisions based on a record that is as complete as possible. To do so, we plan to review and improve our informational services to claimants and to medical providers so that they will better understand what information adjudicators need to make determinations or decisions.

We also are developing requirements for training physicians and psychologists who perform our consultative examinations to make certain that they understand our determination process and the information adjudicators need to make accurate decisions. As part of this effort to improve consultative examinations, we are instituting a quality review to ensure that claimants are getting a good evaluation of their conditions by the right set of eyes and to ensure these examinations are yielding the information we need to make decisions. In addition, we are developing templates that adjudicators will use when they request examinations to ensure that the appropriate information is requested.

Decisional templates are also in the works for adjudicators at the DDS and FedRO levels that will assist them in writing decisions, and we have already started using a decisional template at the administrative law judge level. The use of these templates will help ensure that claims are properly developed, legally sufficient, and consistent with our policies.

The templates are being or have been created and tested with considerable input from adjudicators in the field—the very people who will use them in the new process. They are a critical factor in ensuring accuracy and consistency, and in enabling the quality feedback loops.

In addition, we are working with medical sources to encourage the submission of evidence electronically whenever possible in order to expedite the decisional process. Special arrangements are in place to obtain both medical and non-medical records from large governmental agencies such as the Department of Veterans Affairs, the Military Personnel Records Center, and State Division of Vital Statistics. As a result, Social Security is already the largest repository of electronic medical records in the world. And, we have stringent policies and procedures in place to properly safeguard personally identifiable and medical information from loss, theft, or inadvertent disclosure.

We will begin implementation in the Boston Region for claims filed on or after August 1, 2006. Boston is one of our smallest regions and is comprised of the six States of Connecticut, Maine, Massachusetts, New Hampshire, Rhode Island, and Vermont. After full implementation in these states, we expect to wait an entire year—to monitor the changes and collect management information—before we consider rolling out in a second region.

By taking this careful and measured approach, we will be able to address any issues that may arise and ensure that implementation in future regions will progress efficiently.

Under our implementation plan, DSI will only apply to claims that are filed in a region where the DSI process has been implemented. If a claim is filed in a region where we have not yet implemented the new process, we will use current procedures to adjudicate the claim.

If a claimant moves from one State—where the new process is in place—to another State—that does not have the new process—the adjudicators will apply the regulations that were initially applicable to the claim. In other words, once a claim is under one system, it will stay in that system. This also applies to the pending cases in a region when roll-out begins. Those cases that are already in the system will be worked under the "old" rules and new cases will be worked under the "new" rules.

For example, the elimination of an Appeals Council review will only apply in regions where we have rolled out the new DSI process and to disability claims that have been processed from the start under this rule.

Of course, we will continue to monitor the effects on the disability determination process and the Federal courts as we implement DSI in other regions of the country. Obviously, if we find that there are issues, we will make changes as necessary.

Rollout Begins August 1

As I said, we are rolling out the process on August 1st, and you have my assurance that we are doing all that we can to make sure that we implement in an orderly and timely manner. In typical fashion, the hardworking men and women of SSA and the state DDSs have pulled together and are getting the things done that must be done to move forward.

So far, we have developed major new computer systems to support the DSI initiative. We have performed all of the personnel and hiring work necessary to make sure that we have the new employees in their new positions, properly trained, in time to perform their new DSI duties when implementation begins. We are working to ensure that effective training is prepared and presented to every employee who will be involved with the new disability determination process. Although we do not have the same kind of personnel or hiring issues at the hearing level as we do for other levels, we do have systems needs unique to the hearing level, and we are currently working to ensure that the necessary computer systems are in place by the time the first DSI claim reaches the hearing level.

Conclusion

As you know, shortly after I became Commissioner, I met with President Bush to discuss SSA's disability programs. He asked me three questions:

- Why does it take so long to make a disability decision?
- Why can't people who are obviously disabled get a decision immediately?
- Why would anyone risk going back to work after going through such a long process to receive benefits?

I am proud to say that our new disability process addresses all of these concerns.

As I look back over the long road to the changes we will begin implementing in just a few weeks—and reflect on the spirit of cooperation, professionalism and dedication to serving the public that has been demonstrated by the men and women of SSA and the DDSs, advocacy groups, and Congress—I am convinced that we can make this happen. I am also convinced that the American public will benefit greatly.

As we roll out DSI, we plan to continue the dialogue that has served the process so well. Because this is *not* just about getting it done; it's about getting it done right.

In closing, I want to express again my heartfelt thanks to everyone who has helped us on our journey toward an effective DSI. As I said at the beginning of my testimony today, this subcommittee has traveled with us throughout the journey. I want to thank you again publicly for your advice, insight and support that have meant a great deal to the agency and to me personally. And I know that we can count on your continued support and advice as we make DSI a reality.

Chairman MCCRERY. Thank you, Commissioner Barnhart, and thank you for outlining those changes that you made in response to our concerns and concerns expressed by others.

I mentioned in my opening remarks that on August 1st you're going to start not really a pilot program but a kind of a pilot program. You're going to start in the Boston Region and operate this new system there for 1 year.

What do you hope to learn in that first year? Are you going to try to take things that you learn to modify, at least guide the way for the national rollout?

Ms. BARNHART. I appreciate that question, Mr. Chairman. If I may, I'd like to describe what I call a dynamic management approach to ongoing evaluation and implementation.

There are going to be three facets to what we're going to be monitoring during that first year in particular, and through the whole process, but you asked about the first year.

Specifically, first of all, we're going to be looking at the outcomes.

By that, I mean how many allowances are there, how many denials are there, how soon in the process is it happening, are we really shortening the processing times as we thought, what's happening with the waterfall of cases as a claim moves through each step, are we really making the right decision earlier in the process as we have committed to, what is the effect on the Federal courts, and what is the situation with remands?

All those specific things that we look at now in the system, we're going to be looking specifically in the new process as to how those compare to what's happening today.

Secondly, we're going to be looking at how we are actually implementing the regulation in the way we said we were going to? In other words, are we doing everything we said. If there's an issue and something doesn't seem to be playing out the way we anticipate? Obviously, if we're not implementing it the way we said, we'll be going back to make sure that we do, and taking steps to correct that.

Then finally, if we look at the outcomes and we're implementing the way we said, and we're not getting the results that we anticipated in terms of the right decision as early in the process as possible, then we will certainly be open to revisiting strategic assumptions that we made in crafting this process to begin with.

It's one of the reasons I think the phased-in rollout that we have is important. In fact, we're starting in a smaller region, the Boston Region, a region that has less backlogs, quite frankly, in the hearing offices and will have none by January of this coming year because we're working to move them down.

So, there are a lot of things we're putting in place so that we can get a nice, clean measure of what the situation is going to be in Boston, and we are fully prepared to take action as we move along.

So, we will not be doing a retrospective evaluation, waiting a long time and looking back. We'll be doing it on an ongoing basis, and will certainly be happy to provide information to this Committee as that process plays out.

Chairman MCCRERY. Have you thought about enlisting some outside review organization to look at the results of the first year?

Ms. BARNHART. We did consider that, but because we're not doing an evaluation in the sense of waiting 5 years and then doing a report on it, we really thought that the dynamic approach we're using, that wasn't necessary for us, and it really wouldn't work, because by the time we got the report, we hopefully would have taken action to correct it.

The other thing I would point out is, as you well know, the U.S. government Accountability Office (GAO) who is testifying on the panel that follows me at the request of this Committee, is already looking at how we're doing in terms of implementing the implementation, and I appreciate that, and I really appreciated the GAO report. I read it earlier this week.

I would fully anticipate that that kind of outside oversight would be taking place probably at the behest of this Committee, if not, by GAO's own doing.

Chairman MCCRERY. Okay. In the hearing last year, we talked a little bit about the possible impact on the caseloads of the Federal district courts.

Do you have a plan to measure the impact of this change in the Boston Region?

Ms. BARNHART. We do. In fact, what we're hoping to do is to mitigate any, untoward effects, as far as that goes.

I have worked very closely, and members of my staff have worked very closely with the staff of the Judicial Conference Subcommittee for Disability. Judge McKibben is the head of it. He and I just talked, in fact, just a few weeks ago.

We've had regular contact, trying to make sure we're addressing the issues that they have raised throughout this process. Obviously, they don't want a deluge of cases hitting the Federal courts. We don't, either. We believe if the process works the way we've designed it, we'll see less cases going to the Federal court.

Obviously, we can't stop people from taking cases to Federal court. What I would hope is that we would see fewer meritorious cases going to Federal court because of us doing our job earlier in the process, in other words, that we would see less remands from the court, because we would have done the right job to begin with, we would be pulling back less cases ourselves through what we call voluntary remands.

To ensure that we are doing the best job we possibly can in Boston, we're going to be reviewing 100 percent of the decisions at the Decision Review Board (DRB) before they go on, so that will allow us to actually validate the model that we're going to use as we roll out, for selecting the cases that we would refer to the DRB, and by the way I would point out again it's going to be an equal percentage of allowances and denials, not just one or the other.

Chairman MCCRERY. Lastly, before I turn it over to Mr. Levin for questions, you mentioned the fact that the Boston Region is smaller, and they don't have as much backlog. We're going to have a witness later that's going to talk about how in the Boston Region favorable initial and reconsideration decisions are higher in the Boston Region than nationally.

Does that concern you, that you're using a region that maybe is already a little further along the path to reform, so to speak, or better outcomes.

Ms. BARNHART. Well, let me say this. I was just talking to some of the members who are—the staff that are here with the witness from GAO—and telling them, what I may have told this Committee before, that I came to work in Washington in 1977, and the very first GAO report I ever read was that State allowance rates vary in the DDS disability determinations. That was almost 30 years ago.

It's interesting, it was the first report I read, and I'm here testifying on issues related to that today.

The whole point of creating the Federal reviewing official (FedRO) and creating a centralized quality system as opposed to a regionally based quality system was to ensure consistency across the country, State to State, region to region. We're not going to be doing things based on region or based on State.

In other words, the idea is ultimately when we have this fully implemented, reviewing officials will be looking at cases from all over the country, they won't be doing a particular State. Our quality reviewers will be looking at cases from all over the country, they won't be reviewing a particular State. It should take out any bias that might exist from looking at it on a solely State and regional basis.

In terms of Boston itself, as I said, I chose it for a number of reasons.

First of all, it seems to be less litigious. Less cases go forward to Federal court, and that was important, because obviously we wanted a manageable number, since we're going to review 100 percent of the cases, and they do have a higher allowance rate.

I believe that the approach we're taking with the FedRO, having that Federal review at that very next step, as opposed to the DDS recon, is going to equalize any effects of that.

Chairman MCCRERY. So, you think that the new process you're going to eventually have in place nationwide will actually work to smooth out the differences in allowances among the States?

Ms. BARNHART. I think it will, because we're not going to have—obviously, when you have individuals doing a review, even though you try and make it consistent, you have a certain human variance.

Then you exacerbate that when you have the people in a certain area not under centralized management, where they're getting exactly the same guidance every single day.

Then finally, they become familiar with a particular State.

I think that is just human nature, and the way we do work, it builds certain biases into the system, and that was a real important part of the design, to make sure that we don't have that happening, to equalize that.

Chairman MCCRERY. Okay. Good.

Mr. Levin.

Mr. LEVIN. Let me follow up on that.

You know, sometimes we complain that the opening statements are too long, except if it's Alan Greenspan I guess, but in your case, I'm not sure we gave you enough time.

There are so many of us here. I think the turnout indicates the importance and the interest in this.

So, the discussion of the FedRO, I think, highlights the need for you to describe for all of us, for all of us assembled here, for those who will be watching, what the two or three or four major problems were and how this addresses them, the final regulations.

I think we need to go back a bit——

Ms. BARNHART. I'll be happy to.

Mr. LEVIN. —and have you pick them out and how this addresses it, how you think the FedRO system will work, and so forth, and so forth.

Ms. BARNHART. Okay. First of all, I think in terms of that issue of consistency, Mr. Levin, I appreciate this opportunity, because to me the FedRO is actually really the linchpin of the new process, so I really appreciate this opportunity to elaborate.

I think, as I said to the Chairman, I believe from a consistency perspective, the fact that we'll have Federal employees, not people from 55 different jurisdictions, who are taking a look early in the process from a consistent perspective, is going to be extremely important.

Secondly, from the claimants' perspective, right now, the DDS reconsideration is viewed largely as a rubber stamp of the initial DDS decision. If you ask, there are people here representing claimant representatives and claimant advocacy organizations, and I think most of them would tell you that, and with good reason.

While 40 percent of the cases are allowed—roughly 40 percent, 35 to 40 percent at the initial stage of determination by the DDSs—when it comes to reconsideration, 85 percent of the time, the initial DDS decision is sustained.

Yet what we see is when the cases move on to the hearing level, which is the next stage for reconsideration, the allowance rate is about 63 percent.

So, from the claimants' perspective, I think they will feel first of all, that they're getting a more independent review of their case, which I think is very important. If we're going to take the time for a second step, the claimant and their representatives should know that they're getting a really, truly independent review, and they will not see it so much as a rubber stamp, because if we do our job properly, we'll be documenting the record better all along the way, and we're in the process now of developing, and have completed developments on some of them, templates for the DDSs to use in making their decision and writing their rationale, for the FedRO to use, and we have something called a findings integrated template for the ALJs to use, but all the way through, the record will be better documented.

That means more medical evidence will be gathered, better decisions will be made earlier in the process, which should reduce the number of people who need to go forward to a hearing.

Right now, our hearing process takes over 400-and-some days. That's the average processing time. I wish I could report to you that the time has gotten better since I became Commissioner in terms of the average time. It hasn't. We have actually reduced the time by 4 months if you look at a particular case, but the average time, no, we haven't, because of the volume of cases that are coming in.

For the claimant who is waiting, it's much better for them if they're going to get a "yes" to get it sooner in the process as opposed to have to wait to go all the way through that hearing process to get it.

Mr. LEVIN. So, there's a problem of consistency of effectiveness, would you say, to the older system, the present system, so there wasn't consistency, there wasn't effectiveness, it was—the process you're saying was so that there was allowance and then a rubber stamping of the disallowance and then the overturning of the disallowance, and so that wasn't an effective system, you're saying?

Ms. BARNHART. Correct. Yes. I don't think it is when you have a rubber stamp, essentially rubber stamping.

I'm not taking anything away from our DDSs. Understand they're under tremendous pressure. So, this is really not about them doing a bad job. It's just a system that I think doesn't work when you're reviewing it yourself.

Mr. LEVIN. So, is there another defect that you think is being addressed besides those two?

Ms. BARNHART. Well, I do think development of the record is very important, because I think right now what our ALJs have told me since I became Commissioner is that when they get these records in the hearing offices now, they're not well developed, and oftentimes they have to go all the way back to the DDS to get information. A good part of the delay at the hearing level, Mr. Levin, is the fact that we're having to go back and get things that should have been put in the record before.

By having a decision template that walks you through the logic of what you should have been doing, what you should have been looking at, the factors that should have been considered, and having to write up the logic that you used in coming to the conclusion you came to, it's going to necessitate that you do a better job getting the documents that you should have in the record.

It's a change in orientation from just worrying about initial processing times in terms of speeding it up to making sure that while they're doing the best job they can do, being as efficient as possible, they're actually doing the right thing in terms of documenting the decision, getting the evidence.

We probably could see an expansion of time for initial disability, but ultimately, because less cases would go all the way through, we would see a great savings in time at the hearing level.

Mr. LEVIN. Just one last quick question.

So, what do you think is the most controversial or questionable aspect of this new approach?

Ms. BARNHART. Based on the comments that we received, I would say that the—I hate to use the word controversial, but probably the area that most people expressed concerns about was the elimination of the Appeals Council and the creation of the DRB, and it's one of the reasons that we decided to leave the Appeals Council in effect until the last State is implemented, so the DRB will come up in the new States where we're implementing the new process, but the Appeals Council will continue, as opposed to just eliminating the Appeals Council right off the bat.

It's one of the things that we'll be looking at very closely in terms of what happens with the DRB, our ability to pull the right cases there, to look at them.

What happens, going back to your first question, to the courts, what happens in terms of the workload on the courts. We will be monitoring the DRB very carefully for that reason, because I think that's the area that most people had concerns about.

So, what we're doing is putting in a lot of management information and checks so we know what's going on. We're pledging to monitor and make adjustments as we need to.

Mr. LEVIN. Thank you. Thank you, Mr. Chairman.

Chairman MCCRERY. Mr. Hayworth.

Mr. HAYWORTH. Thank you, Mr. Chairman; and Commissioner Barnhart, welcome back.

Ms. BARNHART. Thank you.

Mr. HAYWORTH. Seeing you here tempts me to wax both nostalgic and rhapsodic about implementation of the first ticket to work in my district back a few years ago, and the efforts to emphasize "ability" in disability.

With your indulgence, I appreciate hearing what is transpiring prospectively, but in real time, there in Tempe and in Arizona, in my State, in Region 9, we've got a little challenge, to put it euphemistically.

Last week, Region 9 management let my State's DDS directors know that they need to reduce the backlog of initial determinations.

In response, the Arizona DDS director apparently ordered a halt to all reconsiderations.

Now, in order for claimants to request a hearing by an SSA ALJ, they must first be denied at the reconsideration level.

From my understanding, the stoppage will only last as long as it takes for the Arizona DDS to reduce the number of initial determinations that are pending, and any initial determination that is disapproved becomes a potential reconsideration case, and with the current stoppage of reconsideration and the focus on initial determinations, it looks like the backlog of reconsiderations can be expected to grow.

Nearly 37 percent of additional determinations are approved for Social Security Disability Insurance (SSDI) or Supplemental Security Income (SSI) benefits, so clearly, focusing no initial determinations will ensure that claimants entitled to benefits will get them as soon as possible.

Unfortunately, those claimants who had been approved on reconsideration will have to wait even longer for benefits, and as I understand it, on average, initial determinations take 95 days and reconsiderations 97 additional days.

How long, if you could estimate it, how do you estimate temporary stoppage of reconsiderations in Arizona to last?

Ms. BARNHART. If I could just explain, we haven't totally stopped reconsiderations anywhere. The dire needs reconsiderations are happening.

It was done—the action that we took was to look at what was going on on a region by region, State by State basis, as you point out your own case in Arizona.

Here's the situation we face. We have now worked almost 9,000 more reconsiderations this year than we have received, which means we got into the ones that came in last year.

The same thing is not true with the initial claims. We're behind. We had 560,000 initial claims pending at the end of last year. We now have 660,000 claims pending right now, where we are, halfway through the year, a little more than halfway through the year.

The reason for that is the subject of this hearing, the hearing that we had just a few weeks ago, which is the fact that we didn't get the allocation the President asked for in the budget, and it meant that we could only replace people at the DDSs, for every two vacancies, one person, so we have not been able to keep the DDS staffed this year the way we would have liked.

So, looking at the fact that we're really ahead in terms of reconsiderations and way behind in terms of initial claims, and it does vary State to State, because obviously population growth, What's really happening in terms of increased workload and so forth affects it, we took a look to try to balance out the workload.

The hope is that it will only be—the way we're looking at it is at the moment, what we're trying to do is direct all available resources, as many as we possibly can, to initial claims.

As this Committee knows, last week, the Congress passed $38 million in the supplemental Katrina appropriation, and I appreciate the support from this Committee. We received $38 million for Social Security, or will in the very near future.

When we sort of repay ourself for what we spent on Katrina, we will then be able to apply that money to increased capacity all across the country.

Obviously, there are going to be limitations on how much capacity at this point, because we're halfway through the year, but I'm going to be monitoring the situation really closely.

What it means, and you actually got to the point of it is, it's not that we're not doing recons, it's that the recons will simply take longer, just like this year, we're restaffing. In some field offices, we have to wait 'til eight vacancies to be able to back fill some positions now, because the funding limitations we have, some people are having to wait longer for an initial appointment to come into a field office to make an application. It's not that we're never going to do them. It's that it's—and that we're not doing them—it's just that it's taking longer to get to them.

I'll be happy to keep you apprised as we look at the situation.

Mr. HAYWORTH. Madam Commissioner, I look forward to that, and I thank you for your time, and I yield back, Mr. Chairman.

Chairman MCCRERY. Thank you, Mr. Hayworth. Mr. Becerra.

Mr. BECERRA. Thank you, Mr. Chairman.

Commissioner, thanks again for being here, and one additional thank you, and that's for the quick response that you and the office gave to the questions that I had raised back at our previous hearing about the adult disabled child issue, and I want to thank you for the quick response.

I know you changed your Web site to address some of those concerns, and I know you're looking for other ways to try to make sure information is received by families that might find themselves in these situations with children and adult children who might be disabled, so thank you very much for that.

Ms. BARNHART. I appreciate you flagging it as an issue for us, because we weren't aware, so we appreciate it.

Mr. BECERRA. Thank you.

Congratulations on moving through the process, and I think sometimes we get down in wanting perfection, and we never get to implement, so I think most of us are looking forward to having a new system up and running and hopefully reducing the backlogs.

Let me just flag some things that I hope you all will continue to monitor, because at this stage, you want to implement, so it's no longer trying to work something out and formulate it, it's implementing.

The FedRO, I think—I hope you will really, as I think has been expressed before, really focus on that, because that's the linchpin to the system.

If that doesn't work, then you're not going to deal with your appeals process very well, because you're still going to have the problem of these decisions not being done well and claimants in the end suffering the consequences.

Late evidence. I know we—you were able to make some changes that I think better accommodate the needs of individuals, but I hope we'll always remember that we don't want to turn these processes, these appeals processes into court hearings. We don't want this to become a court of law where everyone follows these rules of evidence to the tee and you've got an adversarial situation that confronts you so that you can't talk to the other side.

We want the claimants, who for the most part aren't financially well off, to be able to go through a process that's friendly.

So, I hope that when it comes to the issue of evidence, especially late evidence for claimants who, through no fault of their own necessarily, have good late evidence, that that doesn't hurt them.

I also have a concern about how the statutory requirements that say that we must take into account evidence adduced at the hearing will not become an obstacle to considering evidence that comes late.

So, how do you deal with the fact that evidence has to be adduced at the hearing to come to a decision, yet late evidence, which may be critical, comes in, and at what point will we have some appellate decision that tells us, well, you've got a conflict; the statute says you've got to take evidence only that's been only adduced at a hearing versus evidence that's critical and credible that comes in late. So, I hope we continue to monitor that.

Then finally the appellate process. I have some concern about removing that appeals process and going toward these DRBs, but again, I think with have to see them work, and I hope what we do is again not give ourselves a system that becomes like the courts—very formal, very legalistic, very expensive—and we continue to give claimants what they deserve. So, I hope you monitor those things.

The final thing I'll flag for you is something that goes beyond just this whole process, and that's just that you have men and women in your agency who are doing more and more every day, and you have fewer and fewer people doing it, and at some point, you're going to bust. You can't do this.

I know you're limited in what you can say and do, but I hope we will recognize that the work that you do is critical, as critical as any Federal agency or any Federal organ, and unless we have the personnel properly trained and equipped to do this with the ability to have decent morale in the shop, it's all going to fall apart, and you cannot continue to have more imposed upon you and the men and women that work for us without the resources to pay them well and to have the equipment and the materials that you need.

I think more and more we're beginning to see internally that these major backlogs that you've been trying yeomanly to try to address are the result not of any neglect, not as a result of any inexperience, it's just the fact that you don't have enough people, and we've got—I say that to you, and there should be a mirror there, because it really should be said to the Congress. We need to give you the resources you need to do this.

You've got to be honest with us. You've got to let us know, because we hear from a lot of the rank and file in your different offices. It's like what happens with all the social workers who are asked, or the parole officers who are asked to do massive caseloads. You can't do it.

So, I hope that we'll keep that in mind as we move forward, but thank you for the work that you're doing, and we look forward to working with you.

Ms. BARNHART. Thank you. If I could just respond, Mr. Chairman.

Chairman MCCRERY. Sure.

Ms. BARNHART. You've touched on many things. I'm just going to pick a few that I'd really like to comment on.

One of those is the appellate process and the concern you expressed. As I indicated earlier, perhaps that is the area, the elimination of the Appeals Council eventually and the creation of the DRB, where we got the most comments.

One of the changes that we made in the final regulation that we will be monitoring very closely to look at as we roll out to future regions, is that all claimants who move forward—and in Boston it's everybody, because we're going to look at 100 percent of the cases—may submit a statement to the DRB. That is not something that was provided in the NPRM.

What we will be looking at is to see if, as we look at our predictive model and validate it, if the cases where the statement is submitted, where a change was made outside—in other words, the point is to see what the value is of that statement and how we ought to look at institutionalizing, it or changing it, or whatever as we move forward to other regions.

I just want you to know that's one of the reasons we made that change in the final regulation, and we are going to be looking at that very closely, because we're aware of those concerns.

Secondly, in terms of resources, I certainly support what you're saying. I have attempted to be very clear with Congress. Most of those conversations take place at the Appropriations Committee, as you know. This Committee has always been extremely supportive about the resources that we need. That's why I developed the five-year budget plan, to show what you can get for the money.

Just this week, you may be aware that the Appropriations Subcommittee provided $200 million less than was requested in the President's budget, and if I could just take a moment to explain the likely result of that, should that hold.

First of all, that's exactly the amount of money that was set aside in the special funding for the Continuing Disability Review (CDR)s, which means we would not do 237,000 CDRs. During the last time I was here before this Committee just last month, there was a great deal of concern expressed about the CDRs, and recognition that we need to do them.

From a staffing perspective, we would have to cut an additional 1,900 work years, because the elimination of that $200 million, there are people attached to doing that work, and so what that means is the replacement rate we're experiencing now, and in some field offices it is one for every eight vacancies, one person, depending on whether or not there's population growth taking place. In our DDSs it's been one for two. For every two who leave replace one. Those will all change, and it will be even worse than it is now.

So, there are very real consequences, and you're absolutely right. I laid out the backlogs for the hearings. We're looking at backlogs of 660,000 in the DDS. We're trying to get that down to 577,000 before the end of the year.

The point is, not only will we not make headway in terms of working those backlogs away, they will grow even more if we don't get the requested budget that the President made. So, very real terms. We've provided this information to the Committee.

The real, the very real danger, I will be quite candid and tell you is if they do an across-the-board reduction as has been done in the past, say another 1 percent, we may actually be in a position of probably having to furlough staff, for approximately a week.

So, the point is, it's a very serious situation financially for the agency.

Then finally, I would just say your comment about the men and women of SSA, I totally ascribe to your views about the people in this Agency. They do an unbelievable job.

Frankly, if they had not done what they've done in terms of productivity, which means they're working as hard and efficiently as they possibly can, we would be in much worse shape. We've increased productivity by almost 13 percent since 2001. That is due to systems, obviously, but it's also due to the men and women in the agency doing what's necessary to make it happen, too.

Mr. BECERRA. Amen.

Chairman MCCRERY. Ms. Tubbs Jones.

Ms. TUBBS JONES. Mr. Chairman, thank you. I was just fortunate that I decided not to run and get a vote in here before the other group did.

Madam Commissioner, it's always good to see you.

I want to continue down the path about the impact that the 200 million reduction in level of funding will have on the agency. You already talked about it affecting approximately 1,900 workers.

Your plan was to address backlog, so less workers, more backlog. Tell me what impact that will have on your ability to, if you can put it in numbers, to address backlog. You thought you might get through however many cases with this new work. How many cases won't you be able to get through?

Ms. BARNHART. Well, we, as I said, we won't be able to do 237,000 CDRs. That's a very measurable workload.

In terms of turning it into cases, I haven't done that analysis yet, but I'd be happy to do that. We can do that, Ms. Tubbs Jones, and I'd be happy to provide that.

Ms. TUBBS JONES. I'm not a numbers person. I'm just trying to show the real impact that the reduction has. The 237 CDRs shows me what we're talking about.

Ms. BARNHART. I can tell you now, even with level funding in our hearing offices, in other words, we're replacing one for one in our hearing offices. If someone leaves, we replace them. Okay. So, it's a one for—obviously, because of the enormous workload. We still have a workload that's growing this year, if that helps——

Ms. TUBBS JONES. Even when you replace one for one, assume you replace someone with 1 year of legal experience and lose someone with 20 years of legal experience, that's a great, or as big an impact, even if you can do one for one.

Ms. BARNHART. The learning curve issue is huge. We believe it takes about 2 years in our field offices to learn the job and become proficient. In some of the jobs in our hearing offices, it's 2 years.

For our ALJs, and we just brought 41 new ALJs, on we believe it will take 9 months——

Ms. TUBBS JONES. In Cleveland? No, go ahead.

Ms. BARNHART. I can tell you. I knew you'd ask that question.

Ms. TUBBS JONES. Always got to talk about home. We can get that later.

Ms. BARNHART. Actually, we've added, since the last time we talked about this, I've actually, I think added three judges in Cleveland since 2004, but I don't believe there are any scheduled for this time.

There would have been. We were going to hire 100 judges, but because of the budget reductions, we didn't get——

Ms. TUBBS JONES. So, how many less judges are you going to be able to hire?

Ms. BARNHART. We're going to have 59 fewer than we were going to——

Ms. TUBBS JONES. Fifty-nine fewer judges?

Ms. BARNHART. Next year, with the reduction that we're looking at now, if that holds, we probably won't be hiring any judges.

Ms. TUBBS JONES. Talk to me about how many cases a judge generally will handle in any period of time.

Ms. BARNHART. A judge generally handles—well, right now, they're disposing of over two cases a day. At the peak last year,we were at 2.5 cases a day. So, you take 20 workdays a month and you're talking somewhere——

Ms. TUBBS JONES. A significant number.

Ms. BARNHART. Yes, very significant. What is it, 400, 450?

Ms. TUBBS JONES. Significant numbers.

Ms. BARNHART. Yes, very significant numbers. Our judges are carrying enormous caseloads in some areas, sometimes as much as 950 cases per judge.

Ms. TUBBS JONES. Talk to me about the Electronic Disability Folder System (eDib) and the impact it has on the ability to file a claim in a field office.

Ms. BARNHART. Well, eDib, actually, I'm thrilled with eDib. We're in a situation now where every State has electronic disability at different stages of—at different levels.

We have 40 States, though, that now have the ability to work in a fully electronic environment. In other words, they no longer maintain the paper file and the electronic file. They just do the electronic file.

What we're seeing, I can't give you hard numbers now, but I will be able to soon, we're seeing a decrease in the processing time in the States that have electronic disability and we're seeing a real increase in productivity.

If I could just cite a couple of examples—unfortunately I don't have Ohio here, but I do have Illinois, which has moved from 255 cases a month to 279—PPWY of 255 per worker to 279; Idaho from 250 in October to 349 in May; Texas from 261 to 287 in May; and in the Boston Region, where we're going to be implementing first, they've gone from an average of 244 cases to 296 for the month of May.

Ms. TUBBS JONES. Last question. Talk to me about the impact this reduction of $200 million will have on your whole plan of implementing new processes and bringing the agency into a position where they have much less backlog.

Ms. BARNHART. Well, one of the things, as I mentioned, we're trying to get, and we believe we will succeed in getting rid of all backlogs in the Boston hearing offices by January. We'll have pendings, but they won't be backlogs, because you need a certain amount of work to keep working.

My hope is to be able to do that when we move on to Denver, when we move on to Seattle, when we move on to Kansas City, and do as much as we can as we get to the larger regions.

Obviously, if we're not able to backfill people at a one-for-one ratio, and maybe hire some additional people, then we're going to be in a situation of not being able to keep current with the backlogs, let alone work them down, and it's going to make that more difficult.

One of the reasons we have the phased rollout, though, is it will allow us to adapt to whatever the funding situation is, and what it may well mean, Ms. Tubbs Jones, is that we end up having to delay implementation a little bit and stretch it out a little more than the roughly 5 years I project right now.

Ms. TUBBS JONES. Mr. Chairman, thank you very much. Just one more quick thing.

James Hill, will you stand up wherever you are in here? Hi, James Hill, how are you? He is from the great city of Cleveland, Ohio, will be testifying on the second panel, and just in case I don't make it back here, Mr. Chairman, I would for the record welcome a great Buckeye to Washington, D.C. Thank you, Mr. Hill.

Thank you, Mr. Chairman.

Mr. BRADY. [Presiding.] Thank you.

Well, Commissioner, this is an exciting day. I have several questions.

First, let me, Commissioner, thank your folks, your employees at the agency, for two things.

Our district abuts Louisiana, and so we took in tens of thousands of Katrina evacuees, and then when we got hit by Hurricane Rita, we had our own problems. In fact, 10 percent of our evacuees have yet to come back to East Texas, but your local Social Security personnel were just critical, huge help, as we tried to get those people back on their feet and get those benefits reestablished and all their questions answered.

Then secondly, during the rollout of the Medicare prescription drug plan, your folks were especially helpful, not only in the townhalls explaining benefits, also on their own, out there talking to all the senior groups, American Association of Retired Persons (AARP) chapters all that, and toward the end, as seniors were looking to get—to make those decisions, they were very helpful in walking them through the extra program, extra help program and the worksheets and all that.

So, please tell your people they did an excellent job in two categories in our region.

Ms. BARNHART. I will do that, and that will mean a lot to them. They really worked their hearts out. It was a wonderful example, the best I've ever seen of public service, and your comments will mean a lot to them. Thank you.

Mr. BRADY. Great. Thanks.

Another part of the goal sort of like an emergency room that's full of people who can be taken care of in other areas. Part of the goal of this change is to get decisions made accurately and early so we have fewer lining up at the ALJ level of those.

What criteria—what will you consider a success in progress in fewer cases at the ALJ level? How will we view how much progress we've made in that area?

Ms. BARNHART. Yes. I think—we haven't set specific goals or targets at this point, Mr. Brady, but it's a really good question.

I think the first thing I will do is I will look to make sure that the cases that go on to Federal court, the remand rate, in other words, have we reduced the number of the incidents of Federal judges returning cases to us saying, "You didn't do your job right"?

The second thing, I will look at the number of cases that our own attorneys pull back once they've gone to Federal court, what we call voluntary remands, where we, upon review, before going into court to defend a case, actually say, "Wait a minute, we don't think we did our job right."

I will look at what the DRB—the results of the DRB. In Boston we're going to have the luxury of reviewing 100 percent of the cases, to see if they are reaffirming the decisions that are made at the ALJ level, saying, "Yes, we absolutely agree this was the right decision."

I will be looking—basically, what I'm saying is, at each stage, looking back to the stage before, the ALJs, looking to see what they said——

Mr. BRADY. Yes, and I think that's important too, that DDS decision, how many are flowing through the—are their higher rates than should be, larger caseloads than should be, because that's a key.

Ms. BARNHART. So, one of the things, we know we're going to have these feedback loops that go back from each level, but what we're working out now is the vehicle for doing it.

Since the DDSs and the FedROs are different than the ALJs in terms of the fact that they do a review based on our direction and it's not an independent look, like the de novo hearing that the ALJ does, what we're going to do there is probably have our quality, our Office of Quality Performance, which I just created a few months ago, be the conduit for the information for the FedRO to go back to the DDS.

We also, as you know, provide in the regulation to have the ALJ send comments back to the FedRO. What we have to work out there is the vehicle for how that physically happens, how do we actually get them there, but the idea is it's definitely going to go back.

We would like it to be able to go back on an individual basis, but I'm more interested in the aggregate, and I think that speaks to the point that you're making, or the question you're asking, because if I can look and see that in X percent of the comments that went back, the ALJ said, "I agree, you're doing—you made the right decision," if the number of times that the ALJ says to the FedRO, "I think you made the wrong decision," if that decreases over time, then I'll feel like the process is working, because learning is taking place. In other words, the one level is giving feedback and the other level is responding.

Mr. BRADY. Sure.

Ms. BARNHART. I have not set specific numeric goals at this point.

Mr. BRADY. What kind of training are you going to conduct? Obviously this is—that's key, and that I think also is one of the reasons we have disparities between regions and States is that training level.

What have you put in place for that?

Ms. BARNHART. We are doing a lot of training.

In fact, one of our first training sessions happens I think Monday, we start, and we are going to be training executives who are involved in the process inside the Agency, and we have a—in fact, I think today we're doing this—I did a video that's being shown today—it's part of our "Main Streets" series—where I talk about the new process and sort of the big picture for people, and then we move into the specifics next week, and there's more training coming out all the way through July.

We will obviously have to train all of our FedROs, because that position has never existed before, and we have to train people at the DRB.

I have prioritized the training based on the implementation, because obviously our DDSs need to be trained and our field office folks. The DDSs need to receive the first training because that's the first point in the process people hit. They won't hit the FedRO probably for 3 months, two or 3 months after August, and then the DRB will be obviously much later than that.

Mr. BRADY. Right. Are we giving you enough resources for training?

Ms. BARNHART. We feel we're in good shape at this point for training, we do. We can definitely handle that.

Mr. BRADY. I like the idea of this Federal expert unit, and especially bringing in both the medical and occupational, because the change is not so much anymore are you injured, but what type of work can you go back to, so the occupational is key.

Why don't we compel complete and full medical records before the ALJ level? Why don't we compel that before the DDS level? It seems like the more complete the claimant's application is, the better we have of making a good decision early.

Ms. BARNHART. You're absolutely right, and that is really one of the things that we tried to build into this, the incentives for doing that, because the fact is—let's just take a case in point.

If a FedRO overrides a DDS decision, and they do it because of evidence that they got at their stage of the process, that could have been gotten by the DDS, that's the kind of information that's going to go back.

The earlier we decide the case, if it's going to be a yes, the earlier we get to yes, the less expensive it is for us, quite frankly, because it's more expensive at each step administratively, and that thoroughness of having a complete record is one of the absolute goals.

You know, the main goal is to make the right decision as early in the process as possible, but to do that you need to have a complete and well-documented record.

Mr. BRADY. Are there obstacles to completing them earlier in the process, technical obstacles?

Ms. BARNHART. I think one of the things, in all fairness to the DDS, is the pressure that's come on the DDSs in, as long as I can remember for decades, quite frankly, is process the claims faster and faster and faster. You know, do more, do more, do more, and do it faster. I do that to some extent, too.

So, I'm not just talking about former commissioners, all of whom I've known.

What happens is there's a price one pays for that, and what we're trying to say to the DDSs and the culture change that I've talked about many times—I've spoken to the National Association of Disability Examiners (NADE), and to the National Council of Disability Determination Directors (NCDDD), and we'll be doing that again this year, but the main point I'm trying to get across is it may take you a little longer, just like it takes our claims reps longer to do Electronic Disability Collect System (EDCS), in the field office than it did before, but the claim they send to the DDS is a better claim and the DDS spends less time going back and getting information that should have been gotten at the field office.

What I've tried to get across to the DDSs is, I understand you've just been pressured, pressured, pressured, move, move, move the cases. It may take you longer to do what you're supposed to do to develop this record, and to get the medical evidence that needs to be obtained, but in the long run——

Mr. BRADY. You'll save time.

Ms. BARNHART. —the claimant really, what they care about is if their case goes all the way through and because you didn't do it, it takes another 5 months at the hearing level, so we have to look at the whole process, not just in segments.

Mr. BRADY. Okay. Final question.

Obviously, you want to measure the progress on this. One of the frustrations has been trying to, region-to-region, State-to-State, there's just disparities in different areas.

Are you building in a data measurement, a feedback system as it's rolled out in Boston, where we can take a look, more quickly, more accurately compare how the regions are doing, not just in approvals, necessarily, but in time, backlog, negative decisions, feedback.

Ms. BARNHART. Yes. Actually, one of the things that we're trying to do in terms of the variance issue is by creating the FedRO, eliminate the inconsistencies and actually make the process more consistent earlier, and having the FedRO centralized.

I don't mean centralized like in location, although we're starting in Falls Church with this first hiring of FedROs. Eventually, they'll be all around the country in different locations. We can do that because of eDib, but there will be central management of the FedRO, which will get away from this whole notion of this region versus this region and that kind of thing.

So, we're really trying to get rid of the inconsistencies.

In terms of looking at the outcomes that you talked about, though, allowances, denials, processing times, all those kinds of things, we definitely will be tracking that very carefully.

We have a number, a pretty elaborate management information system to collect just about everything I could possibly imagine, although this Committee may well think of something I should have thought of—you seem to always do that. We're doing our best to try and anticipate what you want to know.

We're going to be tracking it for Boston, and obviously we'll be still getting the information we have for the other States, and we'll be able to, look at what the difference is, yes.

Mr. BRADY. Hopefully, that FedRO,—there should be—this is a Federal program. There's naturally going to be some small disparities State to State but there shouldn't be dramatic ones, you know what I mean, if we're going to consistently apply and interpret, throughout the country, and that's been one of the frustrations for everyone in the past.

Before you conclude your testimony, is there anything else you want to add?

Ms. BARNHART. No, just to say again that I really appreciate the interest that this Subcommittee has had in this issue.

It is an undertaking that many people thought was not going to happen because of the nature of what we had to work with, and all the issues and all the interests that come to bear in the disability program, but I do believe that the tone that this Committee sets through its oversight hearings, looking at these issues, goes a long way in promoting the cooperative spirit that I have seen with everybody that I've worked with in the Congress and outside of the Congress, and I think it's something that's seen far too little, it's a far too rare occurrence today.

Mr. BRADY. Right.

Ms. BARNHART. I say that as somebody who came to work in Washington in 1977 to work in the Senate, and so I truly appreciate that level of interest, and I just want you to know that we will continue to provide whatever information you and your staff have, whatever questions that you have. We want to be as responsive as possible.

We believe this can work. We are committed to making it work. We are going to be happy to prove to you that it's working.

If it's not, if something is not working the way it was designed, we are going to step in very quickly to address the issues.

So, thank you.

Mr. BRADY. Right. Well, thank you and good look.

Our next panel will be introduced by the Chairman.

Chairman MCCRERY. [Presiding.] I would invite the next panel to take their seats.

We have Robert Robertson, Director, Education, Workforce, and Income Security Issues with the U.S. government Accountability Office; Marty Ford, Co-Chair, Social Security Task Force, Consortium for Citizens with Disabilities; Sarah Bohr, President, National Organization of Social Security Claimants' Representatives—if we could have a little quiet.

We have Witold Skwierczynski, President, National Council of SSA Field Operations Locals, American Federation of government Employees, AFL-CIO, Baltimore, Maryland; James Hill, President, Chapter 224, National Treasury Employees Union, Cleveland, Ohio; Judge Ronald Bernoski, President, Association of administrative law judges, Sussex, Wisconsin; and Gary Flack, Chairman, Social Security section, Federal Bar Association, Atlanta, Georgia.

Welcome, everyone, and thank you for coming today.

As you heard with our first witness, your written testimony will be submitted for the record in its entirety, and we would like for you to summarize that testimony in about 5 minutes.

You will see in front of you a little box with a green light. When the green light turns to red, that means your 5 minutes has expired and we would like for you to try to wrap up at that time if you haven't already.

We will begin this afternoon with Mr. Robertson.

STATEMENT OF ROBERT E. ROBERTSON, DIRECTOR, EDUCATION, WORKFORCE, AND INCOME SECURITY ISSUES, UNITED STATES GOVERNMENT ACCOUNTABILITY OFFICE

Mr. ROBERTSON. Mr. Chairman, Mr. Levin—do we have a working mic here?

Yes, we do. I'll dispense with the tap, tap, tapping, then.

I'm very happy to be here this morning to discuss SSA's preparations for rolling out its new, revamped disability determination process.

As you're aware, perhaps painfully so, SSA for many years has been struggling to address longstanding problems with its disability claims process in hopes that the DSI process, or DSI, will improve the timeliness and the quality of its disability decisions.

Mr. Chairman, I will make just three points this morning, and in the interests of time and my fellow panel members here, I'll try to do it very quickly.

First, from our perspective, it appears that the actions SSA has taken to help facilitate the successful implementation of the DSI does draw upon many lessons learned from earlier redesign efforts, and I might humbly add also that they reflect a number of our past recommendations.

For example, significant aspects of the DSI rollout are consistent with our recommendations to focus attention on elements that are critical to rollout's success, such as quality assurance and computer supports.

Further, SSA's incremental approach to the rollout, which allows for a year of monitoring and evaluation in one region before expanding the approach to other regions, is also consistent with our past recommendations.

Finally, and fundamental to all of this, SSA's top leadership has shown a commitment to informing affected stakeholders and listening to their advice and concerns with respect to the development and implementation of this process.

This type of two-way communication is of course critical to any successful change management of the magnitude we've been talking about this morning.

The second point I'd like to make is that while SSA has taken many positive steps in preparing for implementing DSI in the Boston region, the rollout schedule is extremely ambitious. As a result, some parts of the rollout strategy are not yet fully developed, including a final plan for its evaluation.

For example, we would hope that SSA has a solid monitoring plan in place once DSI is implemented in Boston. Such a plan is absolutely crucial to quickly identifying and correcting problems that surely will surface during the implementation.

Perhaps more importantly, SSA needs a sound evaluation plan to be in a position of determining whether or not the DSI changes are accomplishing their broader purpose. That is, are they producing more quick decisions, are they producing consistent decisions, that type of thing.

As a quick aside here, I appreciate the questions that came up early in the hearing, talking just about the evaluation plans for this rollout. It is something that every opportunity I get during today's hearing I'm going to emphasize, because I think it's just absolutely critical.

We also hope that SSA's top management will be vigilant in ensuring that communication lines stay open during the critical rollout period in order to fully understand and effectively address questions and concerns that affected stakeholders may have.

My last discussion point relates to the elimination of the Appeals Council and its replacement with a DRB.

Obviously, there's been great concern from a number of stakeholders who in general have noted that the change could increase the workload of Federal courts and additionally results in hardships for claimants in terms of the loss of an administrative appeal level and difficulties associated with pursuing their claims in Federal court.

At this point, Mr. Chairman, we're not in a good position to predict the effects this change will have on Federal court caseloads or on claimants. Obviously, we and many other people in this room will be closely following SSA's assessment of the review board's impact in both of these areas.

I would point out, however, as has been pointed out earlier, that the immediate impact of this change will be somewhat softened by SSA's plan to require that the board review all ALJ decisions in the Boston Region, not just those selected decisions that involve issues that have historically posed challenges to accuracy and consistency.

Mr. Chairman, that ends my prepared remarks and I'll be happy to answer questions at the appropriate time.

[The prepared statement of Mr. Robertson follows:]

Statement of Robert E. Robertson, Director, Education, Workforce, and Income Security Issues, U.S. Government Accountability Office

Mr. Chairman and Members of the Subcommittee:

Thank you for inviting me today to discuss stakeholder concerns about various aspects of the Social Security Administration's (SSA) new Disability Service Improvement process (DSI) and the steps that SSA has taken to address these concerns. SSA is preparing to implement its new process first in its Boston region for at least 1 year beginning in August 2006.

In July 2005, SSA issued a notice of proposed rule making to obtain public comment on DSI proposals that would fundamentally redesign the way claims for disability benefits are processed and considered, with the purpose of improving the accuracy, consistency and fairness of its disability decisions, and making correct decisions earlier in the process. After reviewing comments submitted in response to its notice, SSA issued its final rule in March 2006, codifying many of its proposed changes. One of the many changes envisioned under DSI is the elimination of the Appeals Council, which had afforded claimants the ability to appeal unfavorable decisions made by administrative law judges (ALJ) to SSA before filing suit with a federal court. Once DSI is fully implemented, decisions made by the ALJs become the final agency decision, unless they are selected for review by a new Decision Review Board. The cases selected for review will be those identified through use of a statistical model as claims that are complex or prone to erroneous decisions. As you know, many have expressed concern over the elimination of the Appeals Council as a forum that claimants could avail themselves of before resorting to a federal court.

The information I am providing today is based on work that we conducted between February 22, 2006, and June 2, 2006, as part of ongoing work in this area, in accordance with generally accepted government auditing standards. I will be discussing (1) concerns raised about the replacement of the Appeals Council with the Decision Review Board and how SSA has responded to them, and (2) steps SSA has taken to help facilitate a smooth implementation of the DSI process.

To conduct our work, we reviewed a large sample (252 in total) of the comment letters that were submitted by the public in response to SSA's notice of proposed rule making and that focused on the replacement of the Appeals Council with the Decision Review Board. In addition, we interviewed 10 stakeholder groups—such as claimant representatives, employee groups, and disability advocacy organizations that SSA has previously consulted with—to learn more about their perspectives on the elimination of the Appeals Council as well as on the near-term rollout of the DSI process in the Boston region. In addition, we conducted extensive interviews with SSA officials and reviewed available agency documents to determine their position on and collect data relevant to eliminating the Appeals Council, as well as their efforts and plans related to DSI implementation. Further, we reviewed our past reports on improving SSA's disability process in a number of areas, including human capital; its electronic records system—known as eDib; quality assurance; and implementing change and managing for success. For a more detailed description of our methodology, please see appendix I.

In summary, we found that the public and stakeholders expressed two overriding concerns regarding the replacement of the Appeals Council with the Decision Review board—that the workload of the federal courts will rise if the council is eliminated and that this change will present additional hardship for claimants. In our review of the comment letters submitted to SSA that specifically addressed the elimination of the Appeals Council, we found that about half expressed concern that petitions to federal courts would rise, given the council's termination, and that claimants would lose an additional level of administrative review. About 40 percent of comments highlighted recent improvements in the Appeals Council's processes and noted that eliminating the council would not improve adjudication. Stakeholder groups we spoke with basically underscored these same two points—that eliminating the Appeals Council would result in an increase in disability claims cases that are appealed in federal district courts and that some claimants may drop meritorious claims rather than pursue a seemingly complicated and intimidating federal court appeal. Acknowledging these concerns, SSA contends that DSI will improve decision making earlier in the process, decrease the time it takes the agency to reach a final decision, and reduce the need for appeal. SSA also maintains that because DSI affords claimants the right to appeal their initially denied claims to reviewing officials who are now centrally managed, claimants will not experience an overall loss in administrative review at the federal level. At the same time, both stakeholders and SSA believe it will be important for the agency to closely monitor DSI in order to evaluate its impact on claimants and the courts.

SSA has made substantial preparation for DSI on all fronts related to successful implementation—human capital, technical infrastructure, and quality assurance. However, the timetable is ambitious and much work remains. While stakeholders have expressed concern that SSA will not be able to hire and sufficiently train staff in time for the new process to get under way, we found that the agency has, to date, posted hiring announcements for new positions and developed training packages for onboard staff. SSA is also taking steps, as we had previously recommended, to ensure that key technical supports, particularly the electronic disability system known as eDib, are in place for Boston staff to adjudicate claims under the new process. At the same time, the agency has allowed itself very little time to identify and resolve any potential glitches that may arise before the Boston rollout in August. Regarding quality assurance, SSA has taken several steps to lay a foundation for a more cohesive program, as we had recommended in our earlier reports. For example, features of the new DSI process—including centralizing quality assurance reviews of initial state disability determination service (DDS) decisions, establishing a Decision Review Board for hearing decisions, and developing several tools to aid decision writing—may address problems with decisional consistency that we have identified in the past by allowing for a cohesive analysis of decisions. In addition, SSA officials plan to monitor and evaluate the execution of the Boston rollout, although some performance measures for this initiative, such as for assessing a new medical expert system that is part of DSI, are still unclear to us, and mechanisms for delivering feedback to staff on the clarity and soundness of their decision writing have not yet been fully developed. Finally, SSA is undertaking other, broad steps that we consider consistent with effective change management strategies that we have previously recommended. For example, the decision to implement the new system first on a small scale—that is, in one small region—before introducing it elsewhere should allow for careful integration of the new systems and staff and for working out problems before they become serious impediments to success. Additionally, SSA has employed a proactive, collaborative approach with the stakeholder community in both designing and implementing the new disability determination process.

Background

SSA operates the Disability Insurance (DI) and Supplemental Security Income (SSI) programs—the two largest federal programs providing cash benefits to people with disabilities. The law defines disability for both programs as the inability to engage in any substantial gainful activity by reason of a severe physical or mental impairment that is medically determinable and is expected to last at least 12 months or result in death. In fiscal year 2005, the agency made payments of approximately $126 billion to about 12.8 million beneficiaries and their families. We have conducted a number of reviews of SSA's disability programs over the past decade, and the agency's management difficulties were a significant reason why we added modernizing federal disability programs to our high-risk list in 2003. In particular, SSA's challenges include the lengthy time the agency takes to process disability applications and concerns regarding inconsistencies in disability decisions across adjudication levels and locations that raise questions about the fairness, integrity, and cost of these programs.

The process SSA uses to determine that a claimant meets eligibility criteria—the disability determination process—is complex, involving more than one office and often more than one decision maker. Under the current structure—that is, DSI notwithstanding—the process begins at an SSA field office, where an SSA representative determines whether a claimant meets the programs' nonmedical eligibility criteria. Claims meeting these criteria are forwarded to a DDS to determine if a claimant meets the medical eligibility criteria. At the DDS, the disability examiner and the medical or psychological consultants work as a team to analyze a claimant's documentation, gather additional evidence as appropriate, and approve or deny the claim. A denied claimant may ask the DDS to review the claim again—a step in the process known as reconsideration. If the denied claim is upheld, a claimant may pursue an appeal with an ALJ, who will review the case. At this step, the ALJ usually conducts a hearing in which the claimant and others may testify and present new evidence. In making the disability decision, the ALJ considers information from the hearing and from the DDS, including the findings of the DDS's medical consultant. If the claimant is not satisfied with the ALJ decision, the claimant may request a review by SSA's Appeals Council, which is the final administrative appeal within SSA. If denied again, the claimant may file suit in federal court.

In March 2006, SSA published a final rule to establish DSI, which is intended to improve the accuracy, consistency, and fairness of decision making and to make correct decisions as early in the process as possible. While DDSs will continue to make the initial determination, claims with a high potential for a fully favorable decision will be referred to a new Quick Disability Determination (QDD) process. If the claimant is dissatisfied with the DDS's initial determination or QDD, the claimant may now request a review by a federal reviewing official—a new position to be staffed by centrally managed attorneys. The federal reviewing official replaces the reconsideration step at the DDS level, and creates a new level of federal review earlier in the process. The claimant's right to request a hearing before an ALJ remains unchanged. However, the Appeals Council is eliminated under the new process, and as a result the ALJ's decision becomes the final agency decision except in cases where the claim is referred to the new Decision Review Board. Claims with a high likelihood of error, or involving new areas of policy, rules, or procedures, are candidates for board review. [1] If the board issues a new decision, it becomes the final agency decision. As before, claimants dissatisfied with the final agency decision may seek judicial review in federal court. DSI also includes the introduction of new decision-writing tools that will be used at each adjudication level, and are intended to streamline decision making and facilitate training and feedback to staff. In addition, SSA is creating a Medical and Vocational Expert System, staffed by a unit of nurse case managers who will oversee a national network of medical, psychological, and vocational experts, which are together responsible for assisting adjudicators in identifying and obtaining needed expertise. In its final rule, SSA indicated that DSI will further be supported by improvements, such as a new electronic disability system and an integrated, more comprehensive quality system.

As noted, the changes introduced by DSI were codified in SSA's final rule on the subject. Table 1 highlights these new features and associated elements.

[1] According to SSA, for the first year of implementation in the Boston region, the board will review all ALJ decisions.

Table 1: Key Aspects of DSI

New feature	Associated elements
Quick Disability Determinations	Expedited processing for certain clear-cut cases.
	Use of a predictive model to screen for cases that have a greater likelihood of allowance and to act on those claims within 20 days.
	Nationally standardized training for examiners in DDS on this process.
	Medical or psychological experts must verify that the medical evidence is sufficient to determine that the impairment meets the standards.
Medical and Vocational Expert System	A national network of medical, psychological, and vocational experts who will be available to assist adjudicators throughout the agency.
	The national network will be overseen by a new Medical and Vocational Expert Unit.
	All experts affiliated with the network must meet qualifications, which are still under development.
Federal reviewing officials	A cadre of federal reviewing officials—all attorneys—can affirm, reverse, or modify appealed DDS decisions. Federal reviewing officials cannot remand cases to the DDSs for further review, but they can ask that the DDSs provide clarification or additional information for the basis of their determination.
	Reviewing officials may obtain new evidence and claimants can submit additional evidence at this stage. If necessary, the reviewing official may issue subpoenas for documents.
	If a reviewing official disagrees with the DDS decision, or if new evidence is submitted, he or she must consult with an expert in the expert system.
Decision Review Board	The Decision Review Board will replace the Appeals Council. It will be composed of individuals selected by SSA's Commissioner, and each member will serve a designated term.
	The board will review both allowances and denials, and the board has the ability to affirm, modify, reverse, or remand ALJ decisions.
	A new sampling procedure—or predictive model—will identify ALJ decisions that are error-prone or complex for the board's review. The predictive model, which is still under development, is expected to select 10 to 20 percent of ALJ decisions for the board's review.
	The board has 90 days from the date the claimant receives notice of board review to make its final decision. If it fails to act within that period, the ALJ decision remains SSA's final decision.
	A claimant may submit a written statement to the board within 10 days of receiving notice that the board will review his or her case, explaining why he or she agrees or disagrees with the ALJ's decision. This statement may be no longer than 2,000 words.

Source: GAO analysis.

Note: While DSI does not change the structure or scope of ALJ reviews, the new process has several elements that affect hearings at the ALJ level. Namely, SSA will notify claimants at least 75 days prior to the hearing of the date and time for which the hearing has been scheduled. Additionally, claimants have to submit evidence at least 5 business days before the hearing date itself.

Implementation of DSI will begin on August 1, 2006, in the Boston region, which includes the states of Connecticut, Massachusetts, Maine, New Hampshire, Rhode Island, and Vermont.[2] Therefore, only those claims filed with SSA in the Boston region on or after August 1 will be subject to the new process.[3] All claims currently in process in the Boston region, and claims filed elsewhere, will continue to be handled under current procedural regulations until SSA takes further action.[4] In addition, for cases filed in the Boston region during the first year of DSI implementation, all ALJ decisions—both allowances and disallowances—will be reviewed by a new Decision Review Board with authority to affirm, modify, reverse, or remand decisions to the ALJ.[5] Since DSI will only affect new claims initiated in the Boston region, claimants whose cases were already in process before August—as well as those filing outside the Boston region—will still have access to the Appeals Council.

Concerns Include Fear of Increased Court and Claimant Hardship, while SSA Believes Its New Process Will Reduce the Need for Appeal

In their written comments to SSA and discussions with us, public and stakeholder groups, such as claimant representatives and disability advocacy groups, expressed two broad areas of concern regarding the replacement of the Appeals Council with the Decision Review Board: (1) potential for increasing the workload of the federal courts and (2) anticipated hardship for claimants in terms of loss of an administrative appeal level and difficulties associated with pursuing their claims in federal court. SSA's response to concerns regarding the federal court workload is that all changes associated with new DSI process—taken together—should reduce the need for appeal to the federal courts. At the same time, SSA plans to implement this final step gradually and with additional safeguards to minimize the impact on the courts. In response to concerns about the loss of appeal rights, SSA contends that under the new DSI process, claimants will have a new level of federal review earlier in the process, and should experience a decline in the amount of time it takes to receive a final agency decision without being overly burdened by the Decision Review Board under the new process.

Public and Stakeholders Anticipate a Larger Caseload for Courts, while SSA Maintains That Better Decisions Earlier in the Process Will Reduce the Need for Appeal

Concerns expressed in comment letters to SSA and in our interviews revolved largely around the possibility that the replacement of the Appeals Council with the Decision Review Board would result in rising appeals to the federal courts. Specifically, more than half of the 252 comment letters we reviewed indicated that the Appeals Council provides an important screening function for the federal courts, and that its replacement with the Decision Review Board could result in rising caseloads at the federal court level. Stakeholder groups with whom we spoke reiterated this concern. With the imminent rollout in the Boston region, several stakeholders suggested that SSA closely monitor the effectiveness of the board and the impact of this change on the federal courts.

Data from SSA suggest that the Appeals Council is both screening out a number of cases that might otherwise have been pursued in the federal courts and identifying many claims that require additional agency analysis. Between 2001 and 2005, the number of disability cases appealed to SSA's Appeals Council rose 13 percent. At the same time, the number of disability cases filed with the federal courts (both

---

[2] According to these regulations, SSA will publish a notice in the federal register when it decides to roll out DSI in another region, but this notice will not be subject to the formal rulemaking process.

[3] If a claimant moves to another region from the Boston region, and initially filed the claim in the Boston region on or after August 1, 2006, the conditions of the DSI process will apply to that claimant no matter where he or she moves. If a claimant initially filed elsewhere and then moves to the Boston region, the DSI process will not apply to him or her.

[4] These procedures can be found in the Code of Federal Regulations, 20 CFR 404.900–404.999d and 416.1400–416.1499.

[5] According to SSA, the predictive model used to identify cases that are complex or error-prone will be tested against the board's review of all cases during the rollout in Boston. The model will be tested continually until it has been proven reliable.

DI and SSI) declined 9 percent.[6] Figure 1 illustrates the volume of receipts at both the federal court and the Appeals Council levels during this period.

Figure 1: Federal Court and Appeals Council Receipts between 2001 and 2005

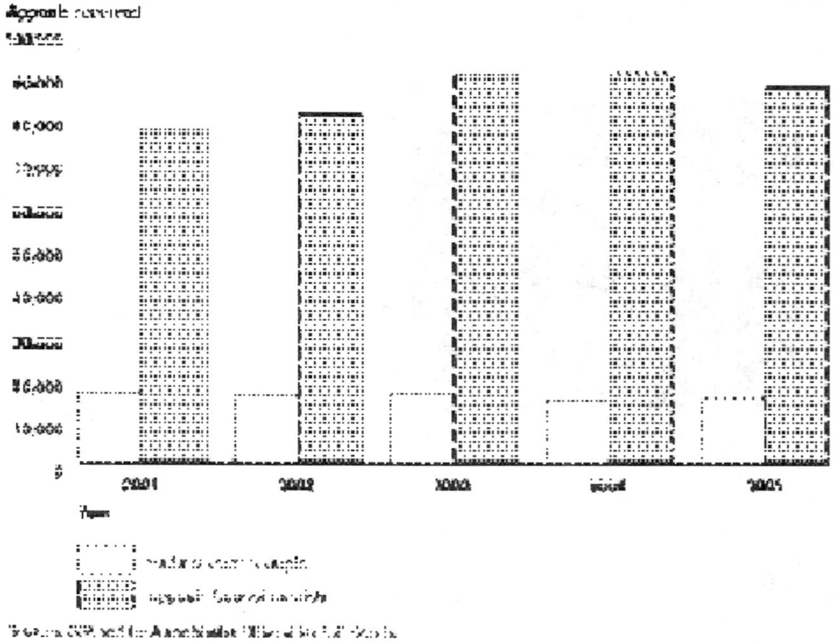

Note: Data on federal court cases are for the 12-month periods ending March 31 of the named year. Data on Appeals Council cases are collected on a fiscal year basis.

Further, the Appeals Council consistently remanded about 25 percent of the claims it reviewed between 2001 and 2005 for further adjudication by the administrative law judge—see figure 2—providing more evidence that the Appeals Council is identifying a significant number of claims that require additional agency review and modification.

[6] According to data from the U.S. District Courts, claims from 15,416 disability insurance cases (both DI and SSI), or 6 percent of the court's total workload, were filed during the 12-month period ending March 31, 2005—down from 16,921 in 2001.

Figure 2: Disposition of Appeals Council Cases, by Fiscal Year, 2001–2005

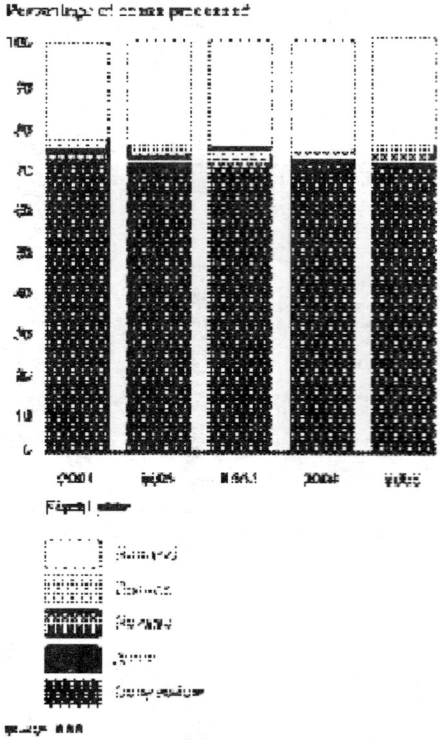

Note: The Appeals Council will deny review if cases do not meet the following criteria—there does not appear to be an abuse of discretion by the ALJ; there is no error of law; the actions, findings, or conclusions of the ALJ are supported by substantial evidence; or the case does not present a broad policy or procedural issue that may affect public interest. If the Appeals Council denies review, the ALJ decision stands as the final agency decision.

SSA believes that the implementation of DSI as an entire process will help it make the correct disability determination at the earliest adjudication stage possible and thereby reduce the need for appeal. According to SSA, several elements of the DSI process will contribute to improved decision making. These include the federal reviewing official position, which presents an enhanced opportunity for the agency to thoroughly review case records—with the assistance of medical and vocational experts—early in the process, as well as new online policy guidance and new tools to aid decision writing, which will be used at each adjudication level to facilitate consistency and help the agency identify and correct errors more quickly. Last, SSA believes that the number of requests for voluntary remands that SSA makes to the federal courts is an indicator that the Appeals Council is not fully addressing errors in the case or otherwise reviewing the case effectively so as to prevent the federal courts from reviewing appeals that should have been handled administratively.[7] SSA believes the Decision Review Board will more effectively screen cases from federal court review by focusing on error-prone claims identified through a predictive model.

SSA acknowledges that the agency cannot predict the likely impact on the federal courts' workload and cannot prevent denied claimants from filing suit with the fed-

[7] According to SSA officials, request for voluntary remands occur when a claimant files an appeal with the federal court and SSA's Office of General Counsel determines that the case is not defensible.

eral courts.[8] To reduce the likelihood of too many appeals reaching the federal court level, SSA stated in its final rule that it is pursuing a gradual rollout by implementing the DSI process in one small region—the Boston region—and plans to have the board initially review all of the ALJ decisions in that region. According to SSA officials, the board's review of all ALJ decisions will allow them to test the efficacy of the new predictive model, to help ensure that the model is identifying the most-error prone cases that might otherwise find their way to federal court. Further, SSA officials told us that they are working with the federal court system to develop a way to gauge changes in the court's caseload. Finally, SSA's internal counsel told us that the agency has begun a systematic data collection process to better understand the circumstances surrounding remands from the federal court. To date, SSA attorneys have analyzed the reasons for federal court remands in more than 1,600 cases, but they are still working on a quality control mechanism to ensure that their information has been entered properly and are therefore unwilling to report on the results of their analysis at this time. [9]

Public and Stakeholders Anticipate Increased Hardship for Claimants, but SSA Believes the New Federal Reviewing Official Position Will Improve Decision Making Earlier

In their comments on the proposed rule and in subsequent conversations with us, stakeholders expressed concern that eliminating the Appeals Council would cause claimants hardship both by eliminating the opportunity to appeal an ALJ decision to the Appeals Council and by increasing the cost and difficulty associated with pursuing cases in federal court.

In particular, 48 percent of the 252 comment letters we reviewed expressed concern that the replacement of the Appeals Council with the Decision Review Board would represent a loss in claimant appeal rights within SSA. These letters, as well as subsequent discussions with stakeholders, emphasized the concern that claimants will not have a say in which cases are reviewed by the board. Further, stakeholders were concerned that in the Boston region, claimants whose cases were allowed at the ALJ level could be overturned by the board, presenting additional hardship for claimants as they await a decision.

In addition, claimant representatives and disability advocacy organizations are concerned that appealing at the federal court rather than Appeals Council level would be costlier and more intimidating for claimants. For example, there is a filing fee associated with the federal courts, and stakeholders commenting on SSA's final rule said that the filing procedure is more complicated than that required for an appeal before the Appeals Council.[10] In addition, claimants seeking representation must find attorneys who, among other requirements, have membership in the district court bar in which the case is to be filed. As a result of these hardships, claimant representatives and disability advocacy organizations, in particular, were concerned that claimants would drop meritorious claims rather than pursue a seemingly complicated and intimidating federal court appeal.

About 40 percent of the comment letters asserted that the amount of time the Appeals Council spent adjudicating cases—also referred to as its processing time—has improved recently, and letter writers did not believe that terminating the Appeals Council would improve the adjudicative process. Although SSA has contended that the Appeals Council has historically taken too much time without providing claimants relief, stakeholders' claims that the Appeals Council processing time has decreased significantly in recent years was confirmed by SSA data—see figure 3. In light of these concerns, many stakeholder groups we spoke with suggested that SSA should roll out the Decision Review Board carefully and closely evaluate outcomes from claimants' perspectives.

---

[8] In the 1990s, SSA conducted a pilot—the Full Process Model—which included, among other changes, eliminating the Appeals Council. According to SSA officials, although they collected some data on the number of direct appeals from the ALJ level to the federal courts, the agency discontinued its pilot before collecting sufficient data for a complete assessment of the model's impact.

[9] SSA officials also indicated that they intend to develop a predictive model, to build on current efforts, that identifies error-prone cases among those denied by ALJs that are subsequently remanded by the federal courts back to SSA for further adjudication.

[10] To appeal to the Appeals Council, applicants need only complete a one-page form and return it to SSA. For the federal courts, there is a $250 filing fee. Although this fee can be waived (based on need), claimant representatives and disability advocates assert that the fee may be cost-prohibitive for some claimants, and representing oneself at the federal court level is challenging.

Figure 3: Appeals Council Processing Time and Volume of Dispositions, by Fiscal Year, 2001–2005

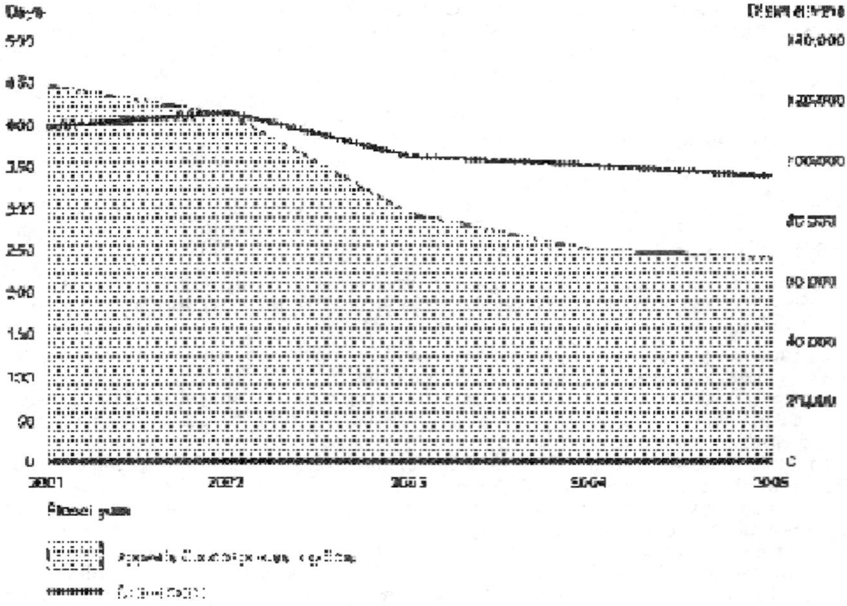

Note: SSA does not track how many of the cases remanded by the Appeals Council result in denials that are appealed again to the council.

In their final rule and in conversations with us, SSA officials stated that the new process still affords claimants comparable appeal rights along with the promise of a faster agency decision. Specifically, SSA stated that DSI includes two federal levels of thorough case development and administrative review—one by the new federal reviewing official and another by an ALJ at the hearings level. SSA contends that the new federal reviewing official position is a marked departure from the reconsideration step, in that the position will be managed centrally and staffed by attorneys specifically charged with enhancing the development of a case and working with a new cadre of medical and vocational experts to make decisions. SSA believes that this new position, along with other changes in the new process, will result in many more cases being correctly adjudicated earlier in the process, resulting in fewer decisions appealed and reviewed by ALJs at the hearings level.

SSA also argues—recent improvements in processing time notwithstanding—that the elimination of the Appeals Council step will reduce the length of time it takes the agency to reach a final decision on behalf of the claimant. Further, SSA maintains that the replacement of the Appeals Council with the board will not be prejudicial to or complicated for the claimant. SSA indicated that claimants will have an opportunity to submit written statements to the Decision Review Board, thus providing another chance to assert their circumstances. SSA maintains that aside from the written statement, further action is not required on the part of the claimant until the board issues its decision.

SSA has told us that it plans to monitor stakeholder concerns in several ways. For example, SSA plans to track the length of time it takes to reach final decisions as well as the allowance rate. SSA also plans to review written statements submitted by claimants to help assess the validity of the board's predictive model.[11]

[11] Specifically, SSA plans to compare the contents of these statements to the results of the predictive model. If SSA determines that using claimant statements will improve the model, SSA would consider revising the model to incorporate information from these documents.

SSA Has Taken Constructive Steps to Implement the New DSI Process, but Its Schedule Is Ambitious and Many Details Are Not Yet Finalized2

SSA has prepared in significant ways for DSI, but the agency's timetable is ambitious and substantive work remains. SSA has moved forward in key areas that should underpin the new system—human capital development, technical infrastructure, and quality assurance. However, some essential measures remain under development, particularly for quality assurance. Nevertheless, on balance, the agency has begun to employ a number of change management strategies we recommended earlier for successful transitioning.

SSA Has Moved to Hire and Train Staff, but It Faces Short Timetables

While stakeholders have expressed concern that SSA will not be able to hire and sufficiently train staff in time for the new process, we found that the agency has taken a number of steps in this area. With respect to hiring for new positions, the agency has already developed position descriptions and posted hiring announcements for nurse case managers, who will work in the new Medical and Vocational Expert Unit, as well as for federal reviewing officials. To date, SSA officials have begun assessing more than 100 eligible applicants for the reviewing official slots, and expect to hire 70 by late June and another 43 in early 2007. SSA officials also said they posted announcements to hire nurse case managers, and that they expect to hire as many as 90 before the end of the rollout's first year in the Boston region.

SSA officials also said that the agency has posted announcements to hire support staff for both the reviewing officials and nurse case managers, but the exact number SSA is seeking to hire has not been decided. Several stakeholders we spoke with were particularly concerned that SSA will need to hire or otherwise provide adequate support staff for reviewing officials to ensure their effectiveness. Specifically, several of the ALJs we interviewed told us that at the hearings level, judges and their staff currently spend significant time developing case files. They noted that if the reviewing official position is designed to focus on case development, then attorneys in this role will need support staff to help them with this time-consuming work.

With respect to training, the agency has been creating a variety of training materials for new and current staff, with plans to deliver training at different times, in different ways. SSA officials reported working on development of a uniform training package for all staff with some flexible components for more specialized needs. Specifically, about 80 percent of the package is common content for all employees, and 20 percent will be adaptable to train disability examiners, medical experts, ALJs, and others involved in the adjudication process. SSA officials said they developed the package with the federal reviewing officials in mind, but also with an eye toward a centralized training content that could apply to current and new staff down the line. SSA plans to provide the full training package, which constitutes about 8 weeks of course work and 13 modules, to reviewing officials in late June, once all attorneys for that position are hired. Among the sessions included are the basics of the disability determination process, eDib and its use, medical listings and their application, and decision writing.

Given that the rule was finalized in March and rollout is set for August, agency timetables for hiring, training, and deploying more than 100 new staff—as well as for training existing examiners—in the six states in the Boston region are extremely short. SSA officials have acknowledged the tight time frame, but hope to deliver training by using more than one medium—in person, online, or by video. SSA still expects to accomplish all hiring and training for the Boston region staff in time for an August 1 launch of the new process.

SSA Has Readied eDib for the Boston Region, but Time for Resolving Last-Minute Glitches before Rollout Will Be Limited

SSA has also taken steps, as we had previously recommended, to ensure that key technical supports, particularly an electronic disability case recording and tracking system known as eDib, are in place in time for Boston staff to adjudicate claims under DSI electronically. The agency has made a variety of efforts to familiarize employees with the system and facilitate their ability to use it as early as possible. First, SSA positioned the Boston region for a fast transition to eDib by reducing the region's paper case backlog. According to a Boston region ALJ, pending case records are being converted now to familiarize judges and decision writers with the eDib system so they will be comfortable with it when new cases reach that level after August 1. Then SSA worked with Boston region staff to certify that the region's DDS offices were ready for full eDib implementation.

According to claimant representatives, SSA has also worked to facilitate their transition to eDib, and according to SSA officials, the agency has developed a system called Electronic Records Express to facilitate medical providers' submission of records to SSA. A stakeholder group of claimant representatives told us that SSA has offered them training and that they have met regularly with agency staff to smooth out eDib issues, such as difficulties associated with the use of electronic folders—electronic storage devices that replace paper folders as the official record of evidence in a claimant's case file. This stakeholders group also reported that its members have voluntarily coordinated with SSA to test new techniques that might further facilitate eDib implementation.

SSA has also been developing electronic templates to streamline decision writing. ALJs have already received some training on theirs, which is known as the Findings Integrated Template. According to SSA officials, this template is now used, voluntarily, by ALJs nationwide, after months of extensive testing and refinement. For DDS-level decisions, SSA is designing a template—called the Electronic Case Analysis Tool (E–CAT)—which it expects to be partially operational by July and fully implemented by November. DDS examiners in the Boston region will receive training on the tool in July and will also receive training prior to then on the elements of sound decision making. A similar tool is in development for the reviewing officials.

While SSA officials expressed confidence in having technical supports sufficiently in place in time for implementation of DSI in August, unanticipated problems associated with new technology may challenge their ability to do so. In addition to eDib and E–CAT, SSA is implementing other new software systems to support the rollout (such as the predictive models and electronic medical records transmission)—any one of which may involve unexpected problems. For example, in 2005 we reported that a number of DDSs were experiencing operational slowdowns and system glitches associated with the new eDib system.[12] It remains to be seen whether the Boston region experiences similar problems with eDib, or problems with other new systems, and whether SSA will be able to resolve technical issues that may arise before implementation begins in August.

SSA Is Improving Its Quality Assurance System as Part of DSI Roolout, although Key Elements Have Yet to Be Revealed

SSA is taking steps to improve its quality assurance system that have potential for improving the accuracy and consistency of decisions among and between levels of review, in a manner that is consistent with our past recommendations. As early as 1999, GAO recommended that in order to improve the likelihood of making improvements to its disability claims process, SSA should focus resources on initiatives such as process unification and quality assurance, and ensure that quality assurance processes are in place that both monitor and promote the quality of disability decisions[13]. Consistent with these recommendations, many of SSA's current efforts involve adding steps and tools to the decision-making process that promote quality and consistency of decisions and provide for additional monitoring and feedback. While these developments are promising, many important details of SSA's quality assurance system have yet to be finalized or revealed to us.

SSA has recently elevated responsibility for its quality assurance system to a new deputy-level position and office—the Office of Quality Performance. This office is responsible for quality assurance across all levels of adjudication. Listed below are new aspects of the quality assurance system that this office oversees and that hold promise for promoting quality and consistency of decisions.

- SSA will continue to provide accuracy rates for DDS decisions, but these accuracy rates will be generated by a centralized quality assurance review, replacing the agency's older system of regionally based quality review boards and thereby eliminating the potential differences among regional reviews that were a cause for inconsistent decisions among DDSs.
- As part of the DSI rollout, SSA plans to incorporate new electronic tools for decision writing to be used by disability examiners, federal reviewing officials, and ALJs. The tools are intended to promote quality in two ways. First, the tools will require decision makers to document the rationale behind decisions in a consistent manner while specifically addressing areas that have contributed to errors in the past, such as failing to list a medical expert's credentials or inaccurately characterizing medical evidence. Second, the tools will help provide a feedback loop, by which adjudicators and decision writers can learn why and

[12] GAO, Electronic Disability Claims Processing: SSA Is Proceeding with Its Accelerated Systems Initiative but Needs to Address Operational Issues, GAO–05–97 (Washington, D.C.: Sept. 23, 2005).

[13] GAO, SSA Disability Redesign: Actions Needed to Enhance Future Progress, GAO/HEHS–99–25 (Washington, D.C.: Mar. 12, 1999).

under what circumstances their decisions were remanded or reversed. SSA officials told us that once the tools are in full use, the Office of Quality Performance will collect and analyze their content to identify errors or areas lacking clarity. They also plan to provide monthly reports to regional managers in order to help them better guide staff on how to improve the soundness of their decisions and the quality of their writing.[14]

- The establishment of the Decision Review Board, with responsibility for reviewing ALJ decisions, is intended to promote quality and consistency of decisions in two ways. First, once DSI is rolled out nationwide, the board will be tasked to review error-prone ALJ decisions with the intent of further ensuring the correctness of these decisions before they are finalized. Second, during the initial rollout phase, SSA plans to have the board review all ALJ decisions to verify that the predictive model used to select error-prone cases is doing so as intended. Importantly, both the tools and the board's assessment are consistent with our prior recommendations that SSA engage in more sophisticated analysis to identify inconsistencies across its levels of adjudication and improve decision making once the causes of inconsistency among them have been identified.[15]

In addition to these actions, SSA told us it plans to measure outcomes related to how DSI is affecting claimants, such as allowance rates and processing times at each adjudication stage, and the proportion of cases remanded from the federal courts and the rationales for these remands. Further, officials told us they will work with the federal courts to track changes in their workload. SSA officials also told us they are working to monitor changes in costs associated with the new DSI process, in terms of both the administrative costs of the process, as well as its overall effect on benefit payments. Officials also said that SSA will track the length of time it takes the agency to reach a final decision from the claimant's perspective, which we have recommended in the past.[16] Although SSA officials told us that ALJ accuracy rates will be generated from the board's review of all ALJ decisions, they said they were not yet certain how they will measure these rates once DSI is rolled out nationwide and the board is no longer reviewing all ALJ decisions.

While these developments are promising, aspects of these changes and of SSA's plans to monitor the DSI implementation have either not been finalized or not been revealed to us. For example, SSA has not yet revealed the types of reports it will be able to provide decision makers based on the decision-writing tools. In addition, while SSA plans to measure the effectiveness of the new process, its timeline for doing so and the performance measures it plans to use have not been finalized. According to SSA officials, potential measures include how well the predictive models have targeted cases for quick decisions at the initial DDS level or error-prone cases for the board, and whether feedback loops are providing information that actually improves the way adjudicators and decision writers perform their work.

SSA Has Employed Other Change Management Practices to Implement DSI

SSA's efforts and plans show commitment to implementing DSI gradually, using tested concepts, involving top-level management, and communicating frequently with key stakeholders—practices that adhere closely to our prior recommendations on effective change management practices.

With regard to gradual implementation, we had previously suggested that SSA test promising concepts in a few sites to allow for careful integration of the new processes in a cost-effective manner before changes are implemented on a larger scale.[17] SSA's decision to implement DSI in one small region is consistent with this recommendation. SSA officials told us they selected Boston because it represents the smallest share of cases reviewed at the hearings level and because it is geographically close to SSA's headquarters to facilitate close monitoring. While SSA officials acknowledged that unanticipated problems and issues are likely to arise with implementation, they assert that they will be able to identify major issues in the first 60 to 90 days. SSA officials believe this will give them plenty of time to make

[14] The purpose of this tool is consistent with GAO's prior recommendations that SSA develop a more focused and effective strategy for ensuring uniform application of SSA's guidance and to improve consistency of decisions. GAO, Social Security Administration: More Effort Needed to Assess Consistency of Disability Decisions, GAO–04–656 (Washington, D.C.: July 2, 2004).

[15] GAO–04–656.

[16] GAO, Observations on the Social Security Administration's Fiscal Year 1999 Performance Report and Fiscal Year 2001 Performance Plan, GAO/HEHS–00–126R (Washington, D.C.: June 30, 2000).

[17] GAO, SSA Disability Redesign: Actions Needed to Enhance Future Progress, GAO/HEHS–99–25 (Washington, D.C.: March 12, 1999) and GAO, Correspondence to Jo Anne Barnhart, Commissioner of the Social Security Administration. (Washington, D.C.: Dec. 19, 2003).

changes before rollout begins in a second region. SSA has also indicated that it plans to roll DSI out next in another relatively small region.

Also consistent with our past recommendations, SSA officials noted that some new elements of DSI have been tested prior to integration. For example, the ALJ tool for decision writing has been tested extensively during development, and they anticipate having fewer challenges when similar tools are used more widely. In addition, SSA has said that it has rigorously tested its model related to the Quick Disability Determination System and that it will continue to check the selection of cases and monitor the length of time it takes for quick decisions to be rendered.

SSA's efforts and plans are also consistent with effective change management practices in that they ensure the commitment and involvement of top management.[18] Specifically, SSA's Commissioner first proposed DSI-related changes in September 2003, and the agency began restructuring itself soon after the rule was finalized. In addition, SSA created a deputy-level post for its new Office of Quality Performance and appointed a new Deputy Commissioner in its newly created Office of Disability Adjudication and Review, which oversees the hearing and appeals processes.

We have also encouraged top managers to work actively to promote and facilitate change, and SSA appears to be adhering to these principles as well.[19] For example, SSA officials told us that the Deputy Commissioners from SSA's offices of Personnel and Human Capital have collaborated with their counterparts in policy units to develop position descriptions and competencies for nurse case managers and federal reviewing officials. According to SSA officials, these leaders are also collaborating to develop interview questions for eligible candidates. Further, SSA officials told us their new human capital plan will be released sometime in July and that it will emphasize the goals of DSI, as well as the personnel changes that will accompany it.

Finally, SSA's communication efforts with stakeholders align with change management principles in several respects. For example, SSA has employed a proactive, collaborative approach to engaging the stakeholder community both during DSI's design and in its planning for implementation in order to explain why change is necessary, workable, and beneficial. Even before the notice of proposed rule making on DSI was published, SSA began to meet with stakeholder groups to develop the proposal that would eventually shape the new structure. Then, once the proposed rule was issued, SSA officials told us they formed a team to read and analyze the hundreds of comment letters that stakeholders submitted. In addition, they conducted a number of meetings with external stakeholders to help the agency identify common areas of concern and develop an approach to resolving the issues stakeholders raised before rollout began. According to SSA officials responsible for these meetings, the Commissioner attended more than 100 meetings to hear stakeholder concerns directly. Further, SSA recently scheduled a meeting for early July with claimant representatives to discuss that group's particular concerns about how the new process will affect their work and their disability clients. SSA officials told us that senior-level staff will lead the meeting and that about 100 claimant representatives from the Boston region will attend.

In addition, SSA officials have also worked to ensure that there are open lines of communication with its internal stakeholders, thereby ensuring that disability examiners and staff in the Boston region are knowledgeable about DSI-related changes. For example, SSA solicited comments and questions from the Boston region's staff about the specifics of the rollout and held a day-long meeting in the region, led by Deputy Commissioners, to respond to these concerns.

Conclusding Observations

For some time, SSA has been striving to address long-standing problems in its disability claims process. From our perspective, it appears that SSA is implementing the new claims process by drawing upon many lessons learned from past redesign efforts and acting on, or at least aligning its actions with, our past recommendations. For example, significant aspects of the DSI rollout are consistent with our recommendations to focus resources on what is critical to improving the disability claims process, such as quality assurance and computer support. SSA's incremental approach to implementing DSI—taking a year to monitor the process and testing new decision-writing tools, for example—is also consistent with our recommendation to explore options before committing significant resources to their adoption. Thus,

---

[18] GAO, Business Process Reengineering Assessment Guide, GAO/AIMD–10.1.15 (Washington, D.C.: May 1997).

[19] GAO/AIMD–10.1.15 and GAO, *Results-Oriented Cultures: Implementation Steps to Assist with Mergers and Organizational Transformations*, GAO–03–669 (Washington, D.C.: July 2, 2004).

the agency is positioning itself to make necessary modifications before implementing the new process in subsequent locations. Finally, and fundamental to all of this, SSA's top leadership has shown a commitment to informing affected stakeholders and listening to their advice and concerns with respect to the development and implementation of this process.

While SSA's steps and plans look promising, we want to stress the importance of diligence and follow-through in two key areas. The first is quality assurance, which entails both effective monitoring and evaluation. A solid monitoring plan is key to helping SSA quickly identify and correct problems that surface in the Boston rollout, because any failure to correct problems could put the entire process at risk. An evaluation plan is critical for ensuring that processes are working as intended and that SSA is achieving its overarching goals of making accurate, consistent decisions as early in the process as possible. The second key area is communication. It is important for SSA's top leadership to support open lines of communication throughout implementation if the agency is to facilitate a successful transition. Failure to, for example, provide useful feedback to staff—many of whom will be new to the agency or at least to the new tools—could significantly jeopardize opportunities for improvement. Just as important, SSA's top management needs to ensure that the concerns and questions of stakeholders affected by the new process are heard, and that concerned parties are kept apprised of how SSA intends to respond.

The eventual elimination of the Appeals Council and its replacement with the Decision Review Board with a very different purpose has been a great cause of concern for a number of stakeholders. SSA appropriately has plans to assess its impact by tracking decisions resulting from each stage of the new process, as well as the effect of the process on the federal courts' caseloads and claimants at large. To its credit, SSA plans to reduce any immediate impact on the courts by requiring that the board initially review all ALJ decisions in the Boston region. However, given that the agency plans to rely heavily on new positions, such as the federal reviewing official, and on new technology, SSA will need to ensure that staff are well trained, and that each adjudicator has the support staff needed to work effectively. Focusing on one small region will, it is hoped, allow the agency to ensure that training, technology, and other resources are well developed to achieve expected goals before DSI is expanded to other parts of the country.

Mr. Chairman, this concludes my prepared remarks. I would be happy to answer any questions that you or other members of the subcommittee may have.

Appendix I: Objectives, Scope, and Methodology

To learn more about the public's and stakeholders' views with regard to the Appeals Council and the Decision Review Board, we reviewed and analyzed a large sample of comment letters they submitted to the Social Security Administration (SSA) in response to its July 2005 notice of proposed rule making on the Disability Service Improvement process (DSI) that were related to these topics. We also interviewed a number of key stakeholder groups to solicit their opinions once the rule had been finalized.

Reviewing and Analyzing Comment Letters

To review and analyze the comment letters, we first downloaded all 1,143 comments that SSA had received and posted to its public Web site. In order to focus our review on only those letters that related to the Appeals Council and the Decision Review Board, we then applied a word search to restrict our analysis to the responses that used the terms "Decision Review Board," "DRB," and "Council."[20] Applying these search terms reduced the number of comment letters for review to 683. We discarded 43 of these 683 letters over the course of our review because they were duplicates of letters by the same authors or did not contain relevant comments. As a result, our final analysis was based on the remaining 640 letters.

To classify the nature of the comments contained in these 640 letters, we coded the opinions as related to one of more of the following concerns:

- The Appeals Council is improving, and its termination will not improve the disability determinations process.
- There is a risk that the Decision Review Board may not select the most appropriate cases for review.
- There is a risk that Decision Review Board could unfairly evaluate or influence administrative law judge decisions.

[20] It is possible that statements could have been made about the Appeals Council and Decision Review Board that did not use these terms, and that we could have missed. If so, the number of responses related to these two entities could be greater than we are reporting.

- In the absence of an Appeals Council, the claimant no longer has the right to initiate subsequent case review.
- There is no opportunity for the claimant or his or her representative to argue before the Decision Review Board.
- A claimant's benefit might be protracted or delayed during Decision Review Board assessment.
- Petitions to the federal court are likely to increase.
- Appeals to the federal court are costly or intimidating, and claimants may not have the wherewithal to pursue the claim at this level.

Of the 640 letters in our review, we initially identified 388 as form letters, or letters containing identical comments, even though they had different authors. To simplify our review, we coded these form letters separately from the other letters. For the 252 letters that we did not initially identify as form letters, one analyst reviewed and coded each letter, while a second analyst verified that he or she had coded the statements appropriately. If the first and second analysts did not come to an agreement, a third analyst reviewed the comment and made the final decision for how the content should be classified. Table 2 below indicates the percentage of the 252 letters citing one or more of the above concerns.

Table 2: Share of Comment Letters Including Each of the Concern Categories Included in This Study

Concern category	Percentage of comment letters expressing concern (n = 252)
Petitions to the federal court are likely to increase.	53
In the absence of an Appeals Council, the claimant no longer has the right to initiate subsequent case review.	48
The Appeals Council is improving, and its termination will not improve the disability determinations process.	38
Appeals to the federal court are costly or intimidating, and claimants may not have the wherewithal to pursue the claim at this level.	37
There is no opportunity for the claimant or his or her representative to argue before the Decision Review Board.	28
There is a risk that the Decision Review Board may not select the most appropriate cases for review.	25
There is a risk that Decision Review Board could unfairly evaluate or influence administrative law judge decisions.	22
A claimant's benefit might be protracted or delayed during Decision Review Board assessment.	18

Source: GAO analysis

For the 388 form letters, we coded one letter according to the process described above. Because the text of the form letters was identical for each, we then applied the same codes to each of the other form letters. All 388 form letters expressed each of the concerns above.

Identifying and Interviewing Stakeholders

To identify key stakeholders, we first referenced the list of organizations that SSA included in its notice of proposed rule making as having met with the agency during its development of the final rule. We then narrowed this list by obtaining suggestions from SSA officials about organizations that are the most active and cover a broad spectrum of disability issues. In total, we spoke with representatives from 10 groups:

- Administrative Office of the U.S. Courts' Judicial Conference Committee on Federal-State Jurisdiction,
- Association of Administrative Law Judges (AALJ),
- Consortium for Citizens with Disabilities' Social Security Task Force (CCD),
- National Association of Councils on Developmental Disabilities (NACDD),
- National Association of Disability Examiners (NADE),

- National Association of Disability Representatives (NADR),
- National Council of Disability Determination Directors (NCDDD),
- National Council of Social Security Management Associations (NCSSMA),
- National Organization of Social Security Claimants' Representatives (NOSCCR), and
- Social Security Advisory Board.

Chairman MCCRERY. Thank you, Mr. Robertson. Ms. Ford.

STATEMENT OF MARTY FORD, CO-CHAIR, SOCIAL SECURITY TASK FORCE, CONSORTIUM FOR CITIZENS WITH DISABILITIES

Ms. FORD. Thank you. Chairman McCrery, Representative Levin, thank you for this opportunity to testify and for your oversight on these important issues.

We applaud Commissioner Barnhart for establishing improvement of the disability determination process as a high priority in her tenure. Her goals of increasing the accuracy, consistency, and fairness of decisionmaking and in turn lessening the need for appeals are critically important.

Millions of children and adults with disabilities rely upon SSI and Title II disability benefits and their related Medicaid and Medicare health services. It is critically important that those who need and qualify for benefits not be forced to wait for months or years to be found eligible.

The implementation of the final regulations must ultimately be measured by its impact on claimants and beneficiaries with disabilities.

The regulations include several major new aspects and also some major changes to long-standing procedures in the process which must be monitored closely. All of these changes and the issues they raise for claimants, their representatives, and adjudicators need to be continuously monitored and studied to determine whether implementation is going as planned and whether there are any unintended consequences for claimants and beneficiaries.

My testimony goes into detail on a number of issues which we believe that SSA must carefully assess and which we urge this Subcommittee to monitor.

While not the subject of the regulations, the new eDib, or electronic file system, is critical to the success of the DSI process, allowing more than one person or people in different locations to work on the case at the same time.

As Commissioner Barnhart has pointed out many times, it is critical that there be better development of evidence at earlier stages in the review of a claim.

The QDD and the medical and vocational expert system are new steps that offer opportunities for improved adjudication if implementation is carefully monitored.

The reviewing official is also a new step, and importantly, the first level for Federal review of an unfavorable decision. The SSA must pay close attention to its careful implementation.

The ALJ level of review has been maintained, but some key elements have been revised. This includes the time limits for submitting evidence and criteria for submission of evidence following the hearing or the decision.

There is no right to appeal to the DRB, the ALJ decision takes on new importance. The SSA should track claimant experience with these changes to ensure that there are no adverse consequences.

Finally, the replacement of the Appeals Council with the DRB could have major implications for claimants and for the Federal courts. Before the DRB replaces the Appeals Council, monitoring the effects of the new process in Region I and making adjustments to protect claimants will be critically important.

The SSA should: ensure that the predictive model is selecting all of the cases with issues that call for administrative remedy, ensure that claimants and representatives receive clear guidelines on the timelines for the DRB and for Federal courts, undertake a thorough review of those cases filed in Federal court to determine whether there has been a failure of the system anywhere along the line, and ensure continuation of the Appeals Council until the DRB has proven successful in the vast majority of cases.

Throughout all of these steps will be the new in-line quality assurance system. It will be important to ensure that the new feedback loops operate properly to continue educating adjudicators about proper evidence gathering and decisionmaking without imposing pressures for predetermined or arbitrary decisions.

The SSA's training efforts at all levels and continued communication with all stakeholders will be important linchpins in whether systems changes will be successful.

In conclusion, we continue to be strongly supportive of efforts to reduce unnecessary delays and to make the process more efficient. By examining the experience in Boston closely within the framework of the goals of accuracy, consistency, fairness, and effectiveness, SSA should aim to ensure appropriate revisions in a timely manner.

The overriding goal is to have the right decision for each claimant, not just a legally defensible decision.

We look forward to continuing work with the Commissioner and SSA and with this Subcommittee as the new process unfolds.

Thank you.

[The prepared statement of Ms. Ford follows:]

Statement of Marty Ford, Co-Chair, Social Security Task Force, Consortium for Citizens with Disabilities

Chairman McCrery, Representative Levin, and Members of the Subcommittee, thank you for this opportunity to testify on Social Security's improved disability determination process.

I am a member of the public policy team for The Arc and UCP Disability Policy Collaboration, which is a joint effort of The Arc of the United States and United Cerebral Palsy. I am testifying here today in my role as Co-Chair of the Social Security Task Force of the Consortium for Citizens with Disabilities (CCD). I also serve as Vice-Chair of CCD. CCD is a working coalition of national consumer, advocacy, provider, and professional organizations working together with and on behalf of the 54 million children and adults with disabilities and their families living in the United States. The CCD Social Security Task Force (hereinafter "CCD") focuses on disability policy issues in the Title II disability programs and the Title XVI Supplemental Security Income (SSI) program.

Let me begin by applauding Commissioner Jo Anne Barnhart for establishing improvement of the disability determination process as a high priority during her tenure. The problems in the disability determination process have evolved over time and are not easy or simple to resolve. Her placing a high priority on improving the system for people with disabilities required dedication and unwavering commitment of her time and critical resources. In addition, we commend Commissioner Barnhart's work in making the Disability Service Improvement (DSI) design process an open one. She has sought the comments of all interested parties, including beneficiaries and consumer advocacy organizations, in response to her initial draft and to the Notice of Proposed Rulemaking. She and her staff have listened to disability community concerns and addressed many of them through changes in the final regulations. We do not agree with all of her decisions, but believe that she has made every effort to understand our perspective and to make her decisions in a fair manner.

We also appreciate Commissioner Barnhart's commitment to continue working with us as the final regulations are rolled out to ensure proper implementation and to make corrections, as necessary, where there are unintended harmful impacts on claimants/beneficiaries.

We thank the Subcommittee for its continuing oversight of these important changes to the disability determination process.

There are numerous areas in the new disability determination process which need to be monitored and studied to determine whether implementation is going as planned and whether there are any unintended consequences from some of the new policies. I highlight the major implementation issues as we currently see them below. Of course, we will continue to raise with the Commissioner and with you any new issues which may arise in the future as implementation proceeds.

As you know, the new regulations will become effective on August 1 in Region 1 (Boston), covering Connecticut, Maine, Massachusetts, New Hampshire, Rhode Island, and Vermont. Commissioner Barnhart has indicated her intention to roll out these changes gradually, monitoring implementation in the Boston region for at least one year before expanding the changes to other regions. We believe that this provides an important opportunity to ensure that implementation is occurring as intended and/or to make corrections to the system to ensure proper implementation.

ELECTRONIC FILES

As you know, the success of the new Disability Service Improvement process is highly dependent on the quality and capacity of the electronic system that will ultimately handle all disability claims in the Social Security Administration. Known as "eDib", this system will make it possible for people in different areas of the country to work on a case at the same time and it will make it possible to eliminate delays caused by loss of case files and from physically sending case files from one location to another. The success of the full implementation of the DSI process will depend on the success and efficiency of the eDib system.

Implementation Issues:

Will claimants/representatives have early access to the electronic files and to new materials added to the files? To know what is in the record at any given point during the process, we believe that optimum meaningful access will ultimately require secure online access with a "read-only" capacity. Will this be available to claimants/ representatives and, if so, when? In the interim, claimants/representatives will need immediate access to information in the file at each administrative level.

Will claimants/representatives be able to obtain hearing recordings immediately after the hearing (particularly if the claimant first acquires a representative after the ALJ hearing)?

SSA should ensure protection of original documents, which are valuable and sometimes irreplaceable evidence, by requiring that exact, unalterable electronic copies of all originals be permanently maintained in the electronic folder. SSA should track whether claimants/representatives experience any problems with having evidence included in the electronic record.

MEDICAL AND VOCATIONAL EXPERT SYSTEM

The rules call for the establishment of a new Medical and Vocational Expert System (MVES) which will provide expert assistance to adjudicators, especially at the reviewing official (RO) and administrative law judge (ALJ) levels of review. The MVES will be composed of the Medical and Vocational Expert Unit and a national network of medical, psychological, and vocational experts who meet qualifications set by the Commissioner.

Implementation Issues

SSA should track:

- The experience of ROs and ALJs with obtaining expert opinions from MVES, including SSA's procedures for ensuring that different experts are used at different levels of review for a claimant's case.

- How MVEU handles cases where the claimant has multiple impairments.
- Use of MVEU for requesting Consultative Examinations.
- Inclusion of treating sources as accepted consultative examiners.

In developing criteria for medical and vocational experts, SSA should ensure that:

- Experts are actively practicing and knowledgeable about the issues, including those requiring a local perspective.
- Criteria for inclusion in the national network are made public.
- Credentials of individual experts are made available to claimants/representatives, for example, through a secure, online source.

SSA should expand the range of expertise available to adjudicators, including occupational therapists, nurse practitioners, physical therapists, registered nurses, psychiatric social workers, and others. Since many of the Listings have a functional component and over half of adult cases are decided on the Listings, such experts, who are trained to evaluate functional limitations and their impact on the ability to work, can help the adjudicators make better decisions.

INITIAL DECISION

As Commissioner Barnhart has pointed out many times, it is critical that there be better development of evidence at earlier stages of the review process. Success in this area is intended to reduce the demand for further review of cases through the appeals process.

The quality of the information/evidence developed for the record will have a significant impact on whether SSA will be able to make the correct decision earlier in the process—one of the Commissioner's key goals for DSI. Asking focused questions of treating sources can elicit information that will be more effective in helping adjudicators reach individualized decisions than a scatter-shot approach which results in much missed, but critical, detail.

In addition, the Commissioner has developed a Quick Disability Determination (QDD) process to ensure that people who are clearly disabled, for whom readily obtainable evidence exists, will move through the process very quickly. A predictive model will identify these claims so that the decisions can be expedited.

Implementation Issues:

SSA will need to determine:

- Whether claimants/representatives are assisted to understand the disability process and what types of evidence need to be obtained.
- Whether providers are given understandable information about what information is needed for adjudication of the claim and whether the Disability Determination Service (DDS) and the RO obtain individualized evidence from the treating sources.

For the QDD process, SSA should track the experience of cases where the QDD unit cannot make a fully favorable determination to ensure that the cases return to the normal DSI process without any adverse consequences to the claimant.

SSA should collect data to indicate how the QDD process compares to decisions of presumptive disability and the TERI (terminal illness) cases.

SSA should collect data on the implementation of the QDD provisions and the predictive model: how many people go through the process; how many are allowed; what impairments they have; etc.

Will the predictive model for the QDD step be public?

FEDERAL REVIEWING OFFICIAL

The federal Reviewing Official level is new in the adjudicatory process. As such, there are many questions about implementation. The RO review will be the first step in the appeals process for claimants. It will also be the first federal level of review for the claimant. Further, it is intended to address the often-raised issues about consistency of decision-making across the country. The RO will not conduct a hearing, but rather will review the developed record and will further develop evidence, as necessary. The RO is a key figure in ensuring that evidence is fully developed and is given subpoena power to gather evidence. The RO level carries a heavy burden in the new DSI and we urge SSA to pay close attention to its careful implementation.

Implementation Issues:

SSA should ensure proper notification of the right to representation and assess whether the earlier notice is resulting in more representation and better development of the record before claimants reach the ALJ level.

SSA must ensure that the requirement to consult with MVEU does not direct a certain type of decision regardless of the individual circumstances. Also, SSA should track whether the RO's required consultation with the MVES results in unreasonable delays in reaching a decision.

SSA must ensure that the claimant can submit evidence up to the time the decision is issued.

SSA should track experience with:

- Review by ROs in a different part of the country from where the claimant lives.
- Whether nationwide consistency (reduction of state-by-state disparity) has improved.
- Processing time at the RO level.

SSA should track the RO use of subpoena power to ensure that evidence is fully developed.

ADMINISTRATIVE LAW JUDGE

The administrative law judge (ALJ) level is not new and the claimant's right to a *de novo* hearing before an ALJ has been preserved. However, there are numerous changes in the procedures, including timeframes for submitting evidence and scheduling hearings. In addition, the ALJ level attains new importance since it may be the claimant's last step in the administrative process (except for an ALJ's dismissal of a hearing), before filing in federal court, if the Decision Review Board (DRB) does not select the case for review. With these changes, SSA's vigilance in monitoring implementation will be critical.

Implementation Issues:

SSA should track experience with the scheduling of hearings:

- Track how many claimants waive notice of 75 days.
- Track claimant experience with objections to time/place of hearing and issues for the hearing.
- Track experience with the rule for submitting pre-hearing evidence 5 business days before the hearing, including tracking denials of a request to submit evidence after the 5 days.
- Track post-hearing evidence submission and decisions about whether the relevant criteria are met.
- Track whether claimants receive a hearing date within 90 days of filing the request for hearing.

Regarding evidence development, SSA should track:

- How many claimants are still missing key evidence from their files when they reach the ALJ level and how that compares to the previous system.
- Whether ALJs meet their own obligations to develop evidence.

Regarding the exceptions for submitting evidence within five business days of the hearing or later, SSA should:

- Ensure ALJ understanding of the requirement to find that the exception criteria are met in delineated circumstances.
- Ensure ALJ understanding of "unavoidable" to include claimant's/representative's inability to acquire evidence from third parties (such as treating source, lab, hospital, etc.).
- Ensure ALJ understanding of the difference between "reasonable possibility" that evidence will "affect" the outcome before the decision is rendered and "reasonable probability" that evidence will "change" the outcome after the decision has been issued.
- Assess whether ALJs are properly applying these standards. If not, what will SSA do to rectify the situation?

SSA should ensure that the findings integrated template (FIT) does not direct decisions in any particular way.

SSA must address how it will ensure a safety net for claimants who experience ALJ bias or misconduct, including SSA's use of the Merit Systems Protection Board procedures.

DECISION REVIEW BOARD

The Decision Review Board is a new entity which follows the ALJ level and replaces the Appeals Council. However, the DRB will be much different than the current Appeals Council. Claimants will have no right to appeal to the DRB. They may submit a written statement upon the request of the DRB or within 10 days of notice that the DRB will review the case. The timelines for decisions by the DRB, the deadlines for filing in federal court, the timelines for an appeal of an ALJ's dismissal of a hearing, and the relationship among all these may prove very confusing to claimants and their representatives.

Since the DRB step is vastly different from the Appeals Council step and the impact on the federal courts is unknown, SSA's careful monitoring of this step in the Boston region will be critically important. For the new DSI process to be successful, SSA should be prepared to address major problems immediately and to consider changes and adjustments as necessary if the impact on claimants and/or the courts is detrimental.

Implementation Issues:

SSA should ensure that claimants/representatives receive clear guidance on the timelines for: submitting a written statement upon the request of the DRB or within 10 days of notice that the DRB will review the case; decisions by the DRB; the deadlines for filing in federal court; the timelines for an appeal of an ALJ's dismissal of a hearing; and the relationship among these deadlines.

During the time in which SSA is reviewing 100 percent of the cases at the DRB level in the Boston region, we think it is important for SSA to:

- Assess the role of the predictive model in detecting the appropriate cases for review—can the model predict the full range of error-prone cases? SSA should examine (1) the cases that the DRB would have reviewed (using the predictive model) against (2) those cases where a significant change was made based on the 100% review but where DRB would not have reviewed the case based on the predictive model.
- Assess the role of the claimant's statement in highlighting the issues for DRB review. SSA should assess the predictive model both with and without the claimant's statements of the case. The results may indicate whether SSA needs to re-assess the role of claimant statements and whether they are critical in raising issues that the predicative model fails to recognize.

Track the results of the 10-day limit on submitting written statements to the DRB, including where a representative or claimant is unavailable during that time, and what impact there may be on the claimant's case if no statement is filed.

Where a representative is new to the claimant, ensure that the representative can get a copy of the hearing recording and the record before the ALJ as soon as possible so as not to miss the 10-day limit for submitting a written statement, or to provide an extension of time.

For those cases which are filed in federal court in the Boston region, undertake a thorough review of the case to determine whether there has been a failure of the new system anywhere along the line.

Ensure continuation of the Appeals Council until the DRB has proven successful in the vast majority of cases.

Track notification of claimants regarding their rights to appeal to federal court.

Other questions:

- How and when will the predictive model be updated? Will the predictive model be made public?
- How will SSA address the Appeals Council's current role in resolving non-disability issues?

FEDERAL COURT

The impact on the federal courts will be a key factor in determining whether the new DSI process is successful. Some of the issues are discussed above regarding the DRB.

Implementation Issues:

In addition to those issues described above regarding the DRB, SSA should:

- Track its experience regarding the number of cases going to federal court to determine whether there is an increase or a decrease.
- Track the number and proportions of SSA's requests for voluntary remands of cases appealed to federal court. Assess the rationale for these requests for voluntary remands and determine whether an earlier failure in the system created the problem.

OTHER/OVERALL ISSUES

There are several procedures/practices which overarch several levels of review. Theses include payments and reimbursement rates to providers; differences in Circuit Court decisions; the new in-line quality assurance systems and feedback loops; issues regarding redaction; operating procedures; and SSA's demonstration authority.

Implementation Issues:

To address these issues, SSA should:

- Ensure that reimbursement rates (ex.: for consultative examinations, copies of records, etc.) are in line with actual costs to providers.
- Ensure that quality assurance feedback loops operate as intended and do not create pressure on the level below to make a certain type of decision regardless of evidence (undue influence).
- Clarify that the requirement that evidence not be redacted applies only to redactions by the claimants/representatives, not to redactions made by the provider (treating physician, lab, hospital, or other treatment source). Redactions that are made by such third party outside of the control of the claimant/representative should not disqualify that evidence for the claimant.
- Where there are acquiescence rulings or differences among the Circuit Courts on an issue, ensure that decision-makers who operate nationwide (or who are not located in the same area as the claimant) apply decisions and rulings properly in the affected regions/states.
- Ensure that the operating procedures are written in a way to ensure the effective and efficient implementation of the final regulations with no unintended consequences or burdens falling on claimants.
- Make operating procedures available to claimants and representatives and include guidance on situations they will newly encounter (such as how to send evidence to the RO assigned to the case).
- Conduct thorough assessments of the demonstration programs (provision of interim minimum health benefits, waiving 24-months waiting period, medical home centers, etc.).

SSA LIMITATION ON ADMINISTRATIVE EXPENSES

I would be remiss if I failed to note the importance of fully funding SSA's Limitation on Administrative Expenses (LAE).

To meet the needs of claimants and beneficiaries during the hurricane emergencies in 2005, SSA was required to redirect $38 million from a budget that had already been reduced $300 million below the President's request for this fiscal year (FY'06). A supplemental appropriation of $38 million, included in the conference report of the supplemental appropriations bill, will help to restore the loss of resources due to the hurricanes so that SSA may continue addressing its substantial on-going workload.

SSA must have the resources to handle its day-to-day work. SSA is a well-managed agency and does a good job with the resources it has been appropriated. However, we have been concerned, and continue to be concerned, that SSA does not have adequate resources to meet all of its current responsibilities, including those of importance to people with disabilities. This includes the need to regularly conduct continuing disability reviews (CDRs). As I understand, the House Appropriations Subcommittee on Labor, Health and Human Services, Education, and Related Agencies has reported a bill that would reduce the President's budget request for SSA's LAE by $201 million, funds which would have been used for conducting additional CDRs. We are hopeful that the full House will ultimately approve a bill that restores the President's full request so that SSA can continue its important work on the disability programs, including conducting CDRs.

ADDITIONAL CONGRESSIONAL ACTION NEEDED

Congress should extend SSA's statutory Title II demonstration authority. Its authority was extended in the Social Security Protection Act of 2004 (P.L. 108–203). The extended authority expired on December 18, 2005, and no new demonstration programs can be initiated.

Conclusion

As stated in our testimony before this Subcommittee in September 2005, while justice delayed can be justice denied, justice expedited also can result in justice denied. As organizations representing people with disabilities, we strongly support efforts to reduce unnecessary delays for claimants and to make the process more efficient. At the end, the goal is to have the right decision, not just a legally defensible decision. We believe it is necessary to examine all of the issues outlined above to assess whether there are any unintended results and to ensure appropriate revisions in a timely manner.

We look forward to continuing to work with Commissioner Barnhart and this Subcommittee as implementation of the new DSI process unfolds.

ON BEHALF OF:

American Association of People with Disabilities
American Association on Mental Retardation
American Council of the Blind
American Network of Community Options and Resources
American Occupational Therapy Association
Association of University Centers on Disabilities
Council of State Administrators of Vocational Rehabilitation
Bazelon Center for Mental Health Law
Inter/National Association of Business, Industry and Rehabilitation
National Alliance on Mental Illness
National Association of Councils on Developmental Disabilities
National Association of Disability Representatives
National Disability Rights Network
National Multiple Sclerosis Society
National Organization of Social Security Claimants' Representatives
National Organization on Disability
National Rehabilitation Association
NISH
Research Institute for Independent Living
The Arc of the United States
Title II Community AIDS National Network
United Cerebral Palsy
United Spinal Association

Chairman MCCRERY. Thank you. Ms. Bohr.

STATEMENT OF SARAH H. BOHR, PRESIDENT, NATIONAL ORGANIZATION OF SOCIAL SECURITY CLAIMANTS' REPRESENTATIVES

Ms. BOHR. Chairman McCrery, Representative Levin, and Members of the Subcommittee, we thank you for the opportunity to testify regarding the changes to the SSA disability determination process known as DSI.

I'm the president of the National Organization of Social Security Claimants' Representatives, the members of which represent claimants in the disability process and are intimately familiar with this process.

We certainly appreciate the Commissioner's willingness to listen to our views and those of other advocates in the disability community.

The final rules reflect a number of changes from the proposed rules which will benefit claimants. However, there are many areas that will require close monitoring by SSA and by claimants and their representatives.

My written statement covers many topics in detail, but today I will focus on three areas that reflect major changes from the current practice: the FedRO; the new requirements for submitting evidence to the ALJ; and the new DRB, and its potential impact on our Federal courts.

The first level of appeal under DSI is to the FedRO, which SSA views as critically important to the new process. Our members have already raised a number of questions about this level which are detailed in my statement.

These concerns include:

Ensuring there will be enough FedROs to handle cases and providing them with sufficient support staff.

Following how many claimants seek representation at the FedRO level.

Are representatives able to effectively communicate with the FedROs and submit evidence?

Does representation earlier in the process lead to better developed cases?

Since FedROs will be required to consult with the medical vocational expert system if they want to allow a claim or if they receive new evidence at the FedRO level, does this requirement cause unreasonable delays and erode the FedRO's authority?

A second key change requires that new evidence be submitted to the ALJ five business days before the hearing. After that, claimants must meet certain requirements to have new evidence considered.

This is a major departure from the current practice that allows evidence, consistent with the Social Security Act, to be submitted at the hearing, if necessary.

This change leaves ALJs with a fair amount of discretion and it needs to be closely monitored by SSA to make certain that eligible claimants are not wrongfully denied benefits.

This is an area of particular concern to representatives, since the ability to obtain medical evidence is often beyond their control.

Some areas for SSA to monitor include:

Tracking the number of requests to submit evidence within the 5 days of the hearing or later and the ALJs' decisions on these requests.

Do denials of requests lead to more district court filings in order for the evidence to be considered by SSA?

Does the DRB pick up erroneously denied requests to submit evidence? Are the rules applied so that claimants who seek representation shortly before a hearing, or even after a hearing, are not improperly disadvantaged?

Are the rules applied in a way that is consistent with the realities of obtaining medical evidence?

The third major change is the elimination of the claimant's right to appeal the unfavorable ALJ decision to the Appeals Council.

Instead, the DRB will screen both favorable and unfavorable ALJ decisions using a "predictive screening tool" that will select "error-prone" cases. If the DRB does not select a case, the claimant will appeal the ALJ decision directly to Federal court.

The SSA recognizes that many groups, including disability advocates and the Federal court judges, are very concerned about the elimination of the Appeals Council step for claimants. This change will require very close monitoring. However, we believe it will take longer than a year to closely monitor and fully assess the impact on our courts.

My written statement outlines a number of statistics that SSA should track, including the disposition of cases by the DRB, the number of court filings by unrepresented claimants, and the number and the types of court dispositions and the underlying reasons.

The SSA also needs to track whether the new rules on ALJ evidence submission affect court filings.

We also have many questions about the "predictive screening tool" and the selection of cases for the DRB review that SSA should evaluate:

Will ALJs be able to learn which cases are more likely to trigger DRB review?

Can a computer-based screening tool identify all of the issues that arise in a case, including subtle issues like ALJ bias or issues specific to the circuit, based on circuit precedent?

We are also concerned about delays in payment of benefits that may arise from the time needed for DRB review of favorable ALJ decisions.

In conclusion, as DSI begins, we'll monitor the process with our members of Region I states and continue to present our concerns to the Commissioner.

Thank you.

[The prepared statement of Ms. Bohr follows:]

Statement of Sarah H. Bohr, President, National Organization of Social Security Claimants' Representatives, Atlantic Beach, Florida

Chairman McCrery, Representative Levin, and Members of the Social Security Subcommittee, thank you for inviting NOSSCR to testify at today's hearing on the Social Security Administration's (SSA) improved disability determination process.

My name is Sarah H. Bohr and I am the president of the National Organization of Social Security Claimants' Representatives (NOSSCR). Founded in 1979, NOSSCR is a professional association of attorneys and other advocates who represent individuals seeking Social Security disability or Supplemental Security Income (SSI) benefits. NOSSCR members represent these individuals with disabilities in legal proceedings before the Social Security Administration and in federal court. NOSSCR is a national organization with a current membership of more than 3,600 members from the private and public sectors and is committed to the highest quality legal representation for claimants. NOSSCR is a member of the Consortium for Citizens with Disabilities Social Security Task Force and we endorse the testimony presented today by Marty Ford on behalf of the Task Force.

I currently am an attorney in a small law firm in Jacksonville, FL, that specializes in Social Security appellate work. Our firm writes briefs for cases before the Appeals Council and in the federal courts, including district courts in over 17 states and six circuit courts of appeals. I also successfully argued a case before the United States Supreme Court, *Sims v. Apfel*, 530 U.S. 103 (2000). I have specialized in Social Security law for over twenty-five years, including 21 years with a legal services program in Jacksonville, where I represented claimants at all administrative and judicial levels, from the initial application through the federal court appellate process. I also am the author of *Bohr's Social Security Issues Annotated*, which surveys Social Security caselaw from all of the federal circuits.

The final regulations on the new Disability Service Improvement process (DSI) were published on March 31, 2006, at 71 Fed. Reg. 16424 (Mar. 31, 2006). The public's interest in these changes can be gauged by the nearly 900 comments that were received in response to the July 27, 2005 proposed rule.

We appreciate the Commissioner's willingness to discuss her proposal and listen to our views. Based on the comments to the proposed rule, the final rule reflects a number of changes, including many that are definite improvements from a claimant's perspective. However, there are many areas that will require close scrutiny by claimants' representatives and that SSA will need to monitor to ensure that the goals of DSI are achieved. My testimony today will discuss these areas of concern, focusing on the Administrative Law Judge (ALJ) and Decision Review Board (DRB) levels.

1. *Implementation of the DSI Process*

DSI will apply only to those claims that are filed in SSA Region I states (Connecticut, Maine, Massachusetts, New Hampshire, Rhode Island, and Vermont) on or after August 1, 2006. Region I will be the only DSI location for at least one year.

NOSSCR is working closely with its members in Region I states to provide ongoing information and support regarding DSI. In July, NOSSCR and the Disability Law Center (DLC) in Boston, MA, will hold an all day seminar in Boston. The goal of the meeting is to provide information and training to Region I members shortly before DSI starts on August 1. Key SSA officials will attend and present updates on DSI implementation. NOSSCR also has worked with DLC to set up a listserve for Region I representatives to share new and updated information about DSI, and to discuss experiences with DSI and issues that will arise. In addition, NOSSCR has created a DSI link on its website, www.nosscr.org, and information also will be posted on a special website maintained by the Disability Law Center, www.masslegalservices.org/cat/3221. Because SSA will follow the process under which the claim was originally filed, we are encouraging our members in non-Region I states to become familiar with the DSI process. Claimants who filed under DSI might move to their states outside Region I and seek representation.

II. *General Issues*

As noted above, NOSSCR is a member of the Consortium for Citizens with Disabilities Social Security Task Force and we endorse and incorporate the issues presented in Marty Ford's testimony today. In particular, we strongly support the need to fully fund SSA's Limitations on Administrative Expenses and give SSA the resources to adequately handle its workload. The Subcommittee is well aware of the increasing delays in processing disability claims. Just last month, the Commissioner testified how cuts in the President's proposed budget for SSA impact the agency's ability to meet its current responsibilities. For DSI to succeed, SSA needs to receive the President's full budget request.

Other DSI issues covered in more detail in the CCD testimony include: better development of the evidence earlier in the process; the Quick Disability Decision process; and the Medical and Vocational Expert System (MVES). There are several other general issues that we would like to mention:

- **What is a "disability claim"?** The DSI regulations state that the new process applies to "disability claims." 20 C.F.R. § 405.1. Many disability claims involve issues which do not strictly deal with the evidence of disability, but are integral parts of the claim, e.g., work-related issues, Title II insured status. They are part of the disability claim and SSA needs to clarify which set of procedures applies.
- **Dealing with two appeals processes.** Most representatives will be trying to manage cases in both the current and DSI processes. And, as described above, it is possible that one client may have issues from the same application in both the DSI and current processes. What will be SSA's policy if an appeal is filed in the wrong system? Will it provide a protective filing date? This problem is not covered by the DSI regulations but needs to be addressed by SSA. Claimants should not be penalized.
- **The electronic folder—eDIB.** NOSSCR generally supports Commissioner Barnhart's technological initiatives to improve the disability claims process, so long as they do not infringe on claimants' rights. The electronic disability folder, "eDIB," has the prospect of significantly reducing delays by eliminating lost files, reducing the time that files spend in transit, and preventing misfiled evidence. We want to thank the Commissioner for her inclusive process to seek comments about the eDIB changes, which will help to ensure that claimants benefit from these important improvements. We have had several very productive meetings and we appreciate this valuable opportunity to provide input.

With electronic folders, claimants' representatives will be able to obtain a single CD that contains all of the evidence in the file. Early access to the record will allow representatives to determine what additional evidence is needed. SSA needs to ensure that access to CDs is available at all administrative levels—the DDS, the Reviewing Official, the administrative law judge, and the Decision Review Board.

Given the need for claimants and their representatives to have access to the file at all levels of the process as early as possible, SSA should explore allowing claimants' representatives to have online access to the files through secure sites, such as those now used by the federal courts. This would free up SSA staff, now providing information about claims, to perform other tasks.

- **Reopening.** In a major change from the proposed rule, the final rule keeps the current reopening rules in place for all claims adjudicated prior to the hearing level. This means that ALJs may reopen decisions at the state agency or RO level and the RO may reopen decisions at the state agency level. However, once an ALJ decision is issued and is the Commissioner's "final decision," reopening of that decision is limited to six months from the date of the decision and "new and material evidence" is not a basis for good cause.

Reopening situations currently do not arise that often, but when they do, they usually have compelling fact patterns involving claimants who did not understand the importance of appealing an unfavorable decision. Often they are claimants who have mental impairments, who previously were unrepresented, or who were unable to adequately articulate their claim in the first application. SSA should monitor subsequent claims at the ALJ and DRB levels to determine whether the DSI reopening rules preclude claimants from eligibility under a prior claim that would be reopened under the current, non-DSI regulations based on "new and material" evidence.

III. *The Federal Reviewing Official*

DSI eliminates the reconsideration level. If a claim is denied at the initial level, the claimant will be informed of the right to appeal to the Federal Reviewing Official (RO). SSA foresees representative involvement at this level by including, for the first time at this early point in the process, information about the right to representation. 20 C.F.R. § 405.115. The notice also will provide more specific reasons and a detailed rationale for the initial denial.

SSA has described the new RO level as the "linchpin" of the DSI process. The RO level will be federal and centrally managed by SSA. ROs will be attorneys who are "highly qualified" and "thoroughly trained in SSA policies and procedures." ROs can be located anywhere in the country since they will be using electronic folders and will not see claimants in person. Initially, all ROs will be located in Falls Church, VA. ROs will handle cases from different states.

The Federal Reviewing Official

- Will staffing at the RO level be adequate? How many ROs will be hired to handle Region I cases? The agency also has stated that it does not want to hire staff attorneys away from hearing offices, since that will cause further problems in those offices. But where else will SSA find attorneys who are "highly qualified" and "thoroughly trained" in SSA policies?
- Will ROs have adequate support staff to assist in their duties, especially, development of the record? What steps will ROs take to fully develop the evidence to create a complete record?
- As authorized by the regulations, will ROs use treating physicians as the preferred source for consultative examinations (CEs)? SSA should track the use of CEs and who performs them.
- Do claimants seek representation at the RO level?
- Are claimants' representatives able to effectively contact ROs? Does representation earlier in the process contribute to better developed records? Can representatives easily communicate with ROs, including both the ability to submit new evidence and the ability to get timely responses from the RO?
- Do RO interactions with the MVES go smoothly? ROs are required to "consult" with the MVES if either new evidence is submitted at the RO level or if the RO disagrees with the DDS's decision, i.e., wants to allow the claim. Will this requirement to consult cause unreasonable delays and/or erode the authority of the RO?
- SSA should maintain statistics on:
  - The number of claimants who are represented at the RO level
  - The time frames for the RO to issue decisions in cases where the RO consulted with the MVES and in cases where no such consultation occurred
  - The frequency with which the MVES agrees or disagrees with the decision of the RO
  - A comparison in the processing times between the RO level and the reconsideration level
  - The allowance rates at the RO level compared with the allowance rates at the reconsideration level
  - The extent to which RO decisions reduce state disparities

IV. *The Administrative Law Judge Level*

The final DSI regulations include provisions that will benefit claimants, including retaining the *de novo* hearing before an administrative law judge (ALJ) and, for the first time, setting a goal (but not requirement) that the claimant receives a hearing date within 90 days after the appeal is filed (although the hearing could be held after the 90 days). SSA should monitor the rate at which the goal of setting the hearing date within 90 days is achieved. Also, the time for providing notice of the hearing date is increased from 20 to 75 days, with the goal of providing adequate time to obtain new evidence. The final rule includes new limits and procedures for submission of evidence. These changes will need to be closely monitored to make sure that claimants who meet the statutory definition of disability are not wrongfully denied benefits.

A. *Submission of Evidence*

The DSI regulations require that new evidence be submitted at least five business days before the hearing. 20 C.F.R. § 405.331(a). After that point, depending on when the evidence is submitted, the ALJ is required to consider the evidence if the claimant meets the specific requirements in the DSI regulations.

The final rule is clearly better than the proposed rule, which required submission at least 20 days before the hearing and had stricter requirements for later submission, but it still represents a major change for practitioners. It also is an area that will require close monitoring to ensure that ALJs correctly apply the regulations, especially in light of 42 U.S.C. § 405(b), which provides that the claimant has the right to a "hearing" with a decision based on "evidence adduced at the hearing." Under pre-DSI regulations that are consistent with the statute, the claimant can submit evidence anytime, including at the hearing. 20 C.F.R. §§ 404.929 and 416.1429.

Under DSI, evidence can be submitted within the 5-business-day period before the hearing, in certain situations. 20 C.F.R. § 405.331(b). The ALJ "**will**" (i.e., "must") accept and consider the new evidence if the claimant shows that: (1) SSA's action misled the claimant; or (2) The claimant has a physical, educational or linguistic limitation that prevented earlier submission of the evidence; or

(3) Some other "unusual, unexpected, or unavoidable circumstance beyond the claimant's control" prevented earlier submission.

These three exceptions form the basis for submission of evidence within 5 business days of the hearing and later. They are the same as the new "good cause" exceptions to extend the time to file an appeal in 20 C.F.R. § 405.20(a). The "good cause" regulation at section 405.20(b)(4) provides the example relevant to efforts to obtain evidence: "You were trying very hard to find necessary information to support your claim but did not find the information within the stated time period."

Based on this statement in the "good cause" regulation, SSA has said that the ALJ must accept new evidence within the 5-day time period if it has been requested but not obtained. In making this statement, SSA relies on the exception in 20 C.F.R. § 405.331(b)(3), i.e., the circumstance beyond the claimant's control, and then refers to the example in 20 C.F.R. § 405.20(b)(4).

However, the evidence submission regulation, 20 C.F.R. § 405.331, does not explicitly reference the good cause regulation, 20 C.F.R. § 405.20, or more specifically, the examples in § 405.20(b). What happens if an ALJ refuses to accept evidence within the 5 day period, even if the exceptions are met? Is there a violation of 42 U.S.C. § 405(b)? SSA says no. But it remains an open question and this area will require very close monitoring.

Submission of evidence after the hearing. *The final rule provides that new evidence can be submitted after the hearing, but under stricter circumstances. Between the hearing and the ALJ decision (and if the ALJ does not hold the record open at the hearing), the requirements for evidence submission are similar to those for submission within 5 days of the hearing. But this rule, 20 C.F.R. § 405.331(c), has an additional significant requirement. The claimant must (1) meet one of the three exceptions discussed above* **and** *(2) show that there is a* **"reasonable possibility"** *that new evidence, alone or with the other evidence, would* **"affect"** *the outcome of the claim.*

After the ALJ decision and if the DRB does not review the ALJ decision, i.e., the ALJ decision becomes the "final decision" of the Commissioner, the claimant may submit new evidence to the ALJ, but with even more additional requirements. Under 20 C.F.R. § 405.373, the claimant must (1) meet one of the three exceptions described above; **and** (2) show that there is a "**reasonable probability**" that new evidence, alone or with the other evidence, would "**change**" the outcome of the decision; **and** (3) file the request with the ALJ within 30 days of receiving the ALJ decision.

Questions to consider:

- What is the actual experience regarding ALJs' consideration of new evidence submitted within five days of the hearing and later? As discussed above, the final DSI rules give ALJs a fair amount of discretion in determining whether to consider new evidence. SSA should track the number of requests to submit evidence within 5 business days of the hearing or later and the ALJ's decision on the request. This information will help determine whether ALJs are following the regulations.

- What happens if an ALJ refuses to accept evidence even if the regulations are met? Does this violate 42 U.S.C. § 405(b) regarding the claimant's right to a decision based on evidence adduced at a hearing?
- Will ALJs' denials of requests to submit new evidence lead to more district court filings? Under 42 U.S.C. § 405(g), the court can remand a case to SSA for consideration of "new" and "material" evidence where there is "good cause" for not submitting it earlier. Will an ALJ's failure to follow the regulations amount to such "good cause"? Will the DRB pick up cases where the ALJ improperly refused to accept new evidence?
- SSA should clarify its policies so that the examples in the "good cause" regulations, 20 C.F.R. § 405.20, also apply to the evidence submission regulations, 20 C.F.R § § 405.331 and 405.373.
- How do ALJs interpret the rule for evidence submission after the hearing, which requires a "reasonable possibility" the evidence would "affect" the outcome? And the rule for evidence submission after the hearing decision, which requires a "reasonable probability" the evidence would "change" the outcome? What is the actual difference between the two standards? "Possibility" vs. "probability"? "Affect" vs. "change"?
- Are the rules implemented in a way that is consistent with the realities of claimants obtaining representation? How are the rules applied if a claimant seeks representation shortly before the hearing? Or within 5 days of the hearing? Or after the hearing is held or the ALJ decision is issued? Based on the experience of our members, claimants who seek and obtain representation shortly before the hearing (or after the hearing) is not an uncommon occurrence since the ALJ hearing is the first in-person contact with an adjudicator (this will not change under DSI).
- Are the rules applied in a way that is consistent with the realities of obtaining medical evidence both before and after the hearing? While we believe the 75-day hearing notice will be a great help, we still anticipate delays in obtaining medical records. We strongly support early submission of evidence; however, our members frequently have great difficulty obtaining necessary records, which is outside their control. While the 75-day notice is a great help, nothing requires medical providers to turn over records within that time period.

B. *The ALJ decision*

The ALJ decision must explain in detail why the ALJ agrees or disagrees with the Reviewing Official's findings and rationale. 20 C.F.R. § 405.370(a). In addition, SSA has developed templates, currently voluntary, for ALJ decisions.

Questions to consider:

- SSA needs to make sure that the decision-making process does not undermine a claimant's right to a *de novo* hearing and that it does not compromise the ALJ's decisional independence. SSA needs to monitor whether the ALJ's obligation to justify disagreeing with the RO interferes with this independence.
- Does any element of the process make it harder for the ALJ to allow a claim than to deny a claim?
- Do ALJs give the RO decision and/or findings any special weight?

C. *Video hearings*

Over the past few years, SSA has held an increasing number of hearings by video teleconferencing. Video hearings provide SSA with management flexibility and administrative efficiency and give SSA a way to balance workloads and help claimants whose local hearing offices have huge backlogs. However, based on our members' experience, SSA has not perfected the video hearing environment and, for many, the video hearing process is not a satisfactory replacement for in-person hearings.

SSA's regulations and policies guarantee claimants an absolute right to decline to appear by video hearing and to request an in-person hearing, so long as the request is timely. The claimant is not required to explain why an in-person hearing is requested. The final DSI regulations reaffirm this right. 20 C.F.R. § 405.315(c).

Questions to consider:

- We continue to hear of instances where ALJs do not follow SSA's regulations and fail to provide an in-person hearing when requested or require a reason for the request. As SSA increases the use of video hearings, the agency needs to make its policy instructions clear regarding the claimant's absolute right to have an in-person hearing and that no reason is required.
- Under DSI, if the claimant objects to the time or place of the hearing, the objections must be made in writing within 30 days of receiving the hearing notice. 20 C.F.R. § 405.317(a). SSA needs to clarify whether a claimant has the same

30-day period to object to a video hearing. Section 405.315(c) does not reference § 405.317(a).

D. *ALJ dismissals*

Under DSI, the only ALJ decision that a claimant can appeal to the Decision Review Board is where the ALJ dismisses the case. These decisions are often legally erroneous but must be addressed before the substantive disability issues can be considered. The DSI regulations require that a claimant first ask the ALJ to vacate the dismissal before asking the DRB to act. However, there is no time limit for the ALJ to act on the request to vacate.

Questions to consider:

- Should there be a time limit for the ALJ to act on a request to vacate a dismissal? After that time limit, the claimant could automatically proceed to the DRB.
- How long does it take ALJs to rule on requests to vacate dismissals? SSA should monitor the length of time it takes ALJs to make decisions on requests to vacate dismissals.
- Is there any change in the rate of dismissals under DSI than under the current regulations? What is the rate at which the DRB overrules the ALJs dismissals under DSI?

V. *Decision Review Board and the Impact on the Federal Courts*

The final rule eliminates the Appeals Council and the claimant's right to initiate administrative review of an unfavorable ALJ decision (other than ALJ dismissals). Instead, the Decision Review Board (DRB) will select cases, both favorable and unfavorable, for own-motion review using a "predictive screening tool" that will identify "error-prone" cases.

In the preamble to the final rule, SSA recognized that many commenters were very concerned about the elimination of the claimant's right to appeal and the impact on the federal courts. As a result, SSA emphasizes several points: implementation will be very gradual; the only claims affected will be those that go through the DSI process from the beginning; the Appeals Council will continue to operate in states where DSI is not implemented (for now, everywhere except Region I) and for all nondisability claims (including Region I states).

The elimination of claimant-initiated administrative review of unfavorable ALJ decisions and creation of the DRB presents one of the major changes under DSI. The DRB process raises many concerns and issues and will require very close monitoring to assess the impact on claimants, on the courts, and on SSA.

A. *Impact on the Federal Courts*

Over the years, the courts have played a critical role in protecting the rights of claimants. We support the current system of judicial review and are pleased that the DSI final rule does not impair that right, except to the extent it could be affected by the procedural change of eliminating claimant-initiated review and significantly increasing the number of court filings. SSA is aware of these concerns, which also have been raised by the Judicial Conference of the United States. While it will be very important to closely monitor the impact of the final DSI changes on the courts, it will be much longer than the one year of Region I DSI implementation before we have any true sense of the impact. And, we may not have a full assessment until after SSA has expanded DSI implementation into another region.

Questions to consider:

- **To assess the impact of eliminating Appeals Council review on the federal courts, SSA should track the following:**
  - Number of ALJ decisions: favorable and unfavorable
  - Disposition of cases by DRB, including the number where it disagrees with the ALJ
  - Number of court filings
  - Number of pro se court filings and number of filings by attorneys
  - Court dispositions, including numbers and reasons for action:
    - Remands: voluntary remands under sentence six of 42 U.S.C. 405(g)
    - Remands: by court decision for errors of law or fact under sentence four of 42 U.S.C.405 (g)
    - Remands: by court decision for new and material evidence and good cause for not submitting earlier under sentence six of 42 U.S.C.
    - Reversals under sentence four of 42 U.S.C. 405(g) Affirmances

- **Do the new rules on evidence submission to ALJs affect court filings?** Additional burdens could be faced by the courts in dealing with new evidence that is submitted to the court but which was not accepted by the ALJ or DRB. Under 42 U.S.C. § 405(g), the court may order that SSA (not the court) take additional evidence if there is a showing that the evidence is new and material and there is good cause for the failure to incorporate the evidence into the record at an earlier administrative level. Claimants may be forced to file an appeal in court just to have SSA consider evidence that should have been considered during the administrative process. As discussed earlier, SSA needs to very closely monitor how ALJs apply the new rules on submission of evidence within five days of the hearing or later. Otherwise, these rules alone could result in a dramatic increase in court filings.
- If federal court filings escalate significantly, will SSA reinstate a final administrative level of review accessible by claimants?
- If the DRB does not complete its review within 90 days of the notice, the claimant can proceed to file in federal court. Will SSA send another notice at the end of the 90 days to inform the claimant that he/she has 60 days to file an appeal in federal court? SSA has said that it will send such a notice, but there is no provision in the final regulations.

B. *Screening ALJ Decisions: The DRB "Predictive Screening Tool"*

Under DSI, the ALJ decision is screened before effectuation. If the DRB decides to review the case, the ALJ decision will only be sent to the claimant with the DRB Notice of review. During the first year of DSI, the DRB will review **all** ALJ decisions in Region I, both favorable and unfavorable. This means that claimants with favorable ALJ decisions will first receive the decision after the DRB screening and with the DRB review notice. And they will not be put in benefits payment status until after the review is completed.

Questions to consider:

- **What is the "predictive screening tool"?** We have been told that SSA and its contractor are looking at recent court decisions, both requests for voluntary remand and court orders, to determine the reasons that the underlying agency final decision was erroneous. A preliminary model will be run to see which cases are picked up. SSA will compare the cases identified by the screening tool to its own hands-on review of cases in Region I. Issues raised in written statements submitted by claimants and their representatives also will be compared to those identified by the screening tool. The process for selection of cases for DRB review raises another series of questions: Will ALJs be able to learn which cases are more likely to trigger DRB review and adjust their decisions accordingly? Does the selection process seem to target certain categories of claimants? By impairment? By functional capacity? By age? Is SSA required to disclose the criteria used in screening?
- **Will screening detect all of the issues that arise in ALJ decisions, including those that are subtle, such as ALJ bias or unfair hearings?** ALJ decisions that are currently reviewed by the Appeals Council often raise a number of legal and factual issues. Is any computer-based screening tool able to identify all of the issues that arise in a case?
- **How will SSA determine whether the predictive screening tool is accurate?** What are the criteria for measuring success? What is an "error-prone" case? Can the model accurately identify "error-prone" cases? What will SSA do if the screening tool does not identify appropriate cases?
- **Will screening be different for ALJ allowances than for denials?** Our members and their clients remain very concerned about delays in payment of benefits that may arise from the time needed for DRB review of favorable ALJ decisions. In Region I, the DRB will not only screen but will review all ALJ decisions, favorable and unfavorable. Claimants will not be put in pay status while waiting for a DRB decision on an ALJ allowance. However, we have been told that SSA is looking at ways to accelerate the screening and review of favorable ALJ decisions, especially dire need cases, TERI (terminally ill) cases, and on-the-record ALJ decisions. Will SSA establish categories of cases where DRB review can be expedited?
- **Does the screening disparately impact certain classes of individuals?** Is there a disparate impact of the screening tool on certain groups of claimants, e.g., those who have a mentally illness? SSA should monitor the selection of cases by the DRB to assure that it is not biased against claimants with specific impairments or who have certain racial or ethnic characteristics.

C. *Written Statements at the DRB*

Written statements can be submitted in every DRB review case (the proposed rule required DRB invitation or permission), but there is a 2000-word limit, about 3 to 4 pages. In Region I, every statement will be part of the DRB review during the first year of DSI implementation, since all ALJ decisions will be reviewed. These written statements from claimants will be extremely important since SSA will want to compare the issues raised in the written statements with those identified by the predictive model. There may be critical information about a case that will only be provided by the claimant and not identifiable from the electronic record.

Questions to consider:

- What criteria will SSA use to determine whether the statements are critical in predicting error-prone cases? If determined that the statements are critical, will SSA change the process?
- Under DSI, the claimant's representative must submit the statement within 10 days after receiving the DRB notice of review, unless the DRB asks for a statement within a set time period. Is the 10-day time limit fair? What happens if a claimant seeks representation after receiving the DRB notice of review? How can the representative obtain a copy of the hearing file and the hearing recording in a timely manner? Will the DRB allow for an extension of the 10 days in appropriate cases?
- Given the importance of the written statements, is an across-the-board limit of 2000 words fair?

D. *Composition of the DRB*

The DRB will be composed of three-member panels. Each panel will have two ALJs and one Administrative Appeals Judge (currently, the members of the Appeals Council). They will serve on a rotational basis and will be appointed by the Commissioner.

Questions to consider:

- How are the panels selected?
- How will SSA ensure that review is fair and neutral? We remain concerned that each panel will have a majority of ALJs who will in turn review the decisions of other ALJs. SSA should establish criteria to guarantee the fairness of the DRB process.

E. *DRB Dispositions*

The DRB is authorized to take certain actions under 20 C.F.R. § 405.440(b):

1. It can affirm the ALJ decision if the ALJ's findings of fact are supported by substantial evidence and/or there is no significant error of law;
2. For errors of law, the DRB can issue its own decision affirming, reversing, or modifying the ALJ decision;
3. For factual findings not supported by substantial evidence and if further development is needed, the DRB will remand to the ALJ.

Under the regulation, remand is the only remedy for factual errors. But what happens if a case has both legal and factual errors? This is not an uncommon occurrence. In many Appeals Council cases I have been personally involved with, the Appeals Council granted review because the ALJ's findings of fact were not supported by substantial evidence; there were errors of law; and new and material evidence was provided. In these cases, he Appeals Council remanded for consideration of the new evidence and for further proceedings. How would the DRB handle the same situation?

F. Submitting Evidence to the DRB

New evidence can be submitted to the DRB, if it reviews a case, under the same requirements as submission of evidence to the ALJ after the decision is issued (and the DRB does not review a case).

However, the regulation, 20 C.F.R. § 405.373(d), does not provide a time frame for submitting the evidence to the DRB. In contrast, after an ALJ decision, new evidence must be submitted within 30 days after the ALJ decision is received.

Questions to consider:

- When should new evidence be submitted to the DRB? Representatives need guidance for the submission of evidence to the DRB. The written statement must be filed within ten days after receiving the DRB notice of review. How does evidence submission coincide with filing the written statement? Is it 30 days after the DRB notice?

- Similar to the concerns about the time limit for submission of the written statement, what happens if a claimant seeks representation after receiving the DRB notice of review? How can the representative obtain a copy of the hearing file and the hearing recording in a timely manner? Will the DRB allow for an extension of the time to submit evidence in appropriate cases, especially where the claimant has undergone medical testing and procedures that are new, material, and related to the alleged disability?

CONCLUSION

For people with disabilities, it is critical that the Social Security Administration address and significantly improve the process for determining disability and the process for appeals. We strongly support efforts to reduce unnecessary delays for claimants and to make the process more efficient, so long as these changes do not affect the fairness of the process to determine a claimant's entitlement to benefits.

As the new Disability Service Improvement process begins, we will monitor the process with NOSSCR members in Region I states and continue to present our concerns to the Commissioner. We believe that communication between claimants' representatives and SSA will play an important role in monitoring DSI implementation and assessing the impact on claimants.

Thank you for this opportunity to testify before the Subcommittees on this issue of critical importance to claimants. I would be glad to answer any questions that you have.

Chairman MCCRERY. Thank you, Ms. Bohr. Mr. Skwierczynski.

STATEMENT OF WITOLD SKWIERCZYNSKI, PRESIDENT, NATIONAL COUNCIL OF SOCIAL SECURITY ADMINISTRATION FIELD OPERATIONS LOCALS, AMERICAN FEDERATION OF GOVERNMENT EMPLOYEES, AFL–CIO

Mr. SKWIERCZYNSKI. Thank you, Chairman, for providing two panels to fit my name. Thank you for the opportunity to testify before the Committee on the commissioner's disability improvement plan.

I represent 50,000 employees, the bulk of the agency, who work on various aspects of Social Security's disability program. The people I represent interview claimants, take and process every single disability claim and appeal that is filed in this agency.

It's the union's belief that the commissioner's disability plan is seriously flawed in many respects and will not achieve the goal of consistency, speed, and a better disability product.

We think staff support is essential. The commissioner alluded to staffing cuts. Last year, the President's budget was reduced, which led to a 2,400 work year reduction. The President's budget this year contains another 2,300 work year reduction.

According to the commissioner's testimony, 2,000 more, 1,900 more would lead to about 6,700 work years over a two-year period reduction in Social Security.

No matter what the commissioner proposes, we cannot sustain those kinds of cuts and provide a good disability product.

The one to eight replacement ratio in the field is outrageous. You will only create a situation where interviews will be backlogged and appointments will be delayed, and there's no way that that will improve the disability process.

The systems changes that are necessary, the commissioner didn't even speak about it, are massive, and unless the proper budgetary support is afforded, they're not going to happen.

The EDCS, our experience with the electronic claims, there was no staff support given to the field and the initial interviews were increased by 20 or 45 minutes, and with no staff support, that obviously led to backlogs.

We applaud the Quick Claims unit idea. Unfortunately, we think that should be done in the field office by Federal claims representatives. There's no need for a handoff. The disability claims manager pilot showed that that can be done right in-house without that kind of a handoff.

We think it's a bad idea to use the best workers in the DDS to do that. They're going to be the easiest claims. What you have left is the less experienced workers doing the tough work that's not involved in the Quick Claims.

With regards to the reviewing official, we have a problem with that person being an attorney. We have no problem with the concept.

We think there's plenty of SSA personnel that are involved in the decision-making process on disabilities who can do that work, and we think it's an insult to them to say that you have to be an attorney to do that.

We think having attorneys in there creates a more litigious process. You have almost every step of the way the claimant dealing with an attorney—at the reviewing official, at the hearing, at the DRB, and in the courts, all attorney-run processes. That is going to create more litigation.

We think the barriers that are put into the process—where the reviewing official has to, in order to overturn a decision, has to have a medical expert opinion; at the next level, for the judge to overturn a decision, he has to write a written rebuttal to the reviewing official; and cutting off the record—are all designed to reduce the disability rolls. There's no doubt in our minds that that's really the goal here, to reduce the disability rolls, and you have barriers in the process that create litigation to arrive at that.

Getting rid of the Appeals Council, there is about a 30 percent remand reversal rate at the Appeals Council, and getting rid of—and obviously, there's a reason for that. The cases either are not fully developed or there's errors. That will be lost in this process.

Closing the record prematurely ensures that people who are disabled and file for disability benefits and don't provide their evidence timely will not get disability benefits, or if they re-file at a later point, they'll lose retroactivity, get lower benefits, it will affect their Medicare, it has massive effects on various aspects of their lives.

We think that what should happen is we should look at the disability redesign approach.

The disability claims manager experiment we thought was very successful.

The adjudicative officer was a little different than the reviewing official, where they were claimant friendly, met with the claimants, met with the attorneys, had the ability to reverse the decision, but also assisted them in preparing for the hearing. We think that's a more claimant friendly approach.

Frankly, neither the commissioner nor the agency has done anything, either in terms of focus groups or in terms of surveys to find out what the claimants actually want, what the public wants, and during the redesign, they did, and the public indicated they wanted a caseworker approach and they wanted to be able to deal with the decisionmaker. This approach here does not get to that point.

Finally, I want to say to the Commissioner, that the employees of Social Security have not really been consulted with regards to this plan, and they're the ones who are best aware of how the process works and what the needs in the system are, and I would urge the commissioner to reestablish communications with the union who represent 50,000 employees so that we can have input on how this plan operates.

[The prepared statement of Mr. Skwierczynski follows:]

Statement of Witold Skwierczynski, President, National Council of SSA Field Operations Locals, American Federation of Government Employees, AFL–CIO, Baltimore, Maryland

Chairman McCrery, Ranking Member Levin, and members of the Social Security Subcommittee, I respectfully submit this statement regarding Social Security's Disability Service Improvement (DSI). As a representative of AFGE Social Security General Committee and President of the National Council of SSA Field Operations Locals, I speak on behalf of approximately 50,000 Social Security Administration (SSA) employees in over 1500 facilities. These employees work in Field Offices, Offices of Hearings & Appeals, Program Service Centers, Teleservice Centers, Regional Offices of Quality Assurance, and other facilities throughout the country where retirement, survivor and disability benefit applications and appeal requests are received, processed, and reviewed.

SSA employees are dedicated to providing the highest quality of service to the public in a compassionate manner. AFGE represents employees who are committed to serving communities in the face of a significant increase of work and decrease of staff. However, the severe cuts in budget and staff have had a detrimental effect on employee morale and, also, the ability for SSA to fulfill public service demands.

Although SSA's workloads have increased by 12.6 percent over the last 5 years, and 2.7 percent in FY 05, Congress appropriated $300 million less for SSA than proposed in the President's FY06 budget request. The result was a 2368 reduction in budgeted work years. While SSA's proposed budget requests have compared favorably compared to many other agencies, AFGE is concerned that the recent budget cuts may result in dangerous levels of inadequate service to the public and stewardship of the programs under SSA's jurisdiction.

In February 2006, SSA informed AFGE that the budget cuts would be absorbed in staffing resources. Since then, Commissioner Barnhart imposed a hiring reduction wherein the Agency will replace only *1 of 8* employees engaged in direct public service work in field offices who leave SSA. These are the employees who interview disability and disability appeals applicants.

AFGE is very concerned that such staffing cuts will drastically affect SSA's ability to provide adequate public service to the disabled community. AFGE also raises a number of questions regarding the decisions to reduce direct service staffing. Why are such cuts necessary if SSA has the resources to implement Disability Services Improvement (DSI) which is a system that has never been tested and will cost billions of dollars to implement? If there are insufficient Claims Representatives and Technical Experts to take and process initial claims, all the DSI improvements in the world won't improve the system. The entire system requires sufficient staffing resources on the front end to enable the public to file applications for disability benefits that fully address the nature of their condition, their medical sources and how their disability impacts their ability to work and to perform routine tasks. There is currently insufficient staff to do this job. Commissioner Barnhart's staff replacement plan will further reduce the staff that processes disability claims. Flooding the appellate system with dollars while slicing the staff that takes applications makes no sense and is not an effective way of improving the system.

Commissioner Barnhart's Disability Service Improvement Plan

AFGE continues to be very concerned about the Commissioner's plans to move forward with her disability initiative.

The record should be clarified with regards to Commissioner Barnhart's statement that she met with the organizations that represent SSA employees. She did. She held one meeting with all 6 SSA AFGE presidents for the purpose of introducing her plan. That was 3 years ago. Ms. Barnhart was not receptive to our constructive criticisms. The leadership of six bargaining councils has more than 150 years of specialized experience with SSA and represents 50,000 bargaining unit employees. She refused to include experienced bargaining unit employees in strategy sessions or workgroups that helped design the new plan. The Union rejected this plan and Ms. Barnhart has since refused to meet and/or discuss any subject matter with AFGE. The AFGE Local in the Boston Region has yet to be informed of any implementation plans of DSI. However, she has decided to meet with 2 minor unions that represent less than 10 % of SSA employees regarding her plan. They support it. AFGE doesn't. Her failure to meet with representatives of employees who process disability claims every day and, consequently, understand the disability process is dangerous and may lead to adverse repercussions for the entire disability claims system.

Ms. Barnhart does not have the support or the buy-in of SSA workers. In fact, SSA employees overwhelmingly oppose this disability plan.

Currently 55 million Americans have a disability, of which 8.3 million Americans and their families receive Social Security Disability Insurance (SSDI) (17.1% of all Social Security benefits are paid to disabled beneficiaries and their families.) Some disabilities are long term (e.g., broken back) while others are permanent (e.g., blindness, quadriplegia).

Processing time for hearings appeals has dramatically increased. Prior administrations attempted to develop different methods to streamline the disability determination process. Some pilot projects, such as the Disability Claims Manager, were considered to be successful (i.e., resulted in applicants receiving benefits twice as fast) and were overwhelmingly supported by the public. However, Commissioner Barnhart refused to implement those pilots and instead developed a new, untested approach to alter the process. It is the Union's belief that the Commissioner's approach will do little to get benefits to the disabled applicant faster or improve service. The commissioner's plan eliminates one appeal step and implements new legal barriers to obtaining benefits:

- The rules provide for the establishment of a Quick Claims Unit for claims filed by individuals who have obvious disabilities. Claims that are sent to this unit are required to have a completed disability decision within 20 days. The union favors the establishment of such a unit. The union opposes placement of the unit in the State Disability Determination Service (DDS). This is an unnecessary handoff. Employees who work in SSA field offices are entirely capable of being trained to make such disability determinations. The DCM pilot proved that fact. SSA public surveys indicate that there is an overwhelming desire from the public that disability decisions should be made by the person who interviews them. The Quick Decision Units provide the Agency with an opportunity to streamline the process by eliminating a handoff and, at the same time, satisfy the public desire for a caseworker to be empowered to decide both the disability and non-disability portions of their claim. Allowing federal employees in field offices to make disability decisions would require Congress to change the exclusivity portions of the law that currently reserve such decisions to the state. It is time for Congress to enact such a change in the law and improve public service. Sending these obvious disability approval cases to DDS units who will be staffed by the best DDS Disability Examiners will also adversely affect the rest of the disability workload. Assigning less experience personnel to process the toughest cases where the decisions are not clear cut, is a recipe for disaster. The best employees should work the most difficult cases—not the easiest.
- In place of the current Reconsideration process, attorneys (Federal Reviewing Officials) will review cases and write a "legal decision" that will serve as the SSA's legal position on the case. In spite of the Commissioner's hiring freeze for direct service positions and her claim of budget shortages, an army of attorneys are being hired as this statement is written. The trust fund (SSA) and general revenue (SSI) impact of eliminating reconsiderations currently processed in the DDS and replacing them with a reviewing official attorney is unknown. Failure to pilot this change is risky and reckless. Substantial deviation from the current disability approval rates could lead to unwarranted expenditures or, conversely, more stringent policy decisions regarding the definition of a disability. In addition, it appears that the substitution of attorneys for State DDS Disability Examiners will result in substantially more administration expenses. Congress should be careful to ask SSA for projected costs of this change both on administrative expenses and benefit outlays.

Although the regulations were silent on the issue of cost analysis, it would be crucial for Congress to request that SSA track the costs associated with the Federal Reviewing Official, including the costs associated with clarification and developmental requests to State DDSs and medical providers as well as the processing time, accuracy, case costs, allowance rates, and appeal rates.

It is also unclear as to the rules that the Federal Reviewing Official would be utilizing in making his/her decision (i.e. listings, case law, judgment, etc.). This would have to be identified in any comparison if the Federal Reviewing Officials utilize different rules than that of the State DDSs.

- The Administrative Law Judge (ALJ) will now be limited in what he/she can consider as evidence from the claimant as all medical evidence must be presented five days prior to the hearing. The ALJ is limited in what he/she can consider good cause for late medical evidence notwithstanding its relevance. Prior to the Commissioner's new approach, the ALJ was allowed total discretion to accept and evaluate evidence. Under the new rules, the ALJ's written decision must explain in detail why he/she agrees or disagrees with the substantive findings and overall rationale of the Federal Reviewing Official's legal decision. The ALJ must rebut SSA's legal decision if benefits are to be awarded to a claimant. One can anticipate that hearing reversal rates will decrease due to the pressure on the ALJ to uphold the Reviewing Official decision. Claimants that currently are approved for legitimate disabling conditions will be denied under Commissioner Barnhart's system because of the premature closing of the record. Does Congress actually want a system where their constituents are denied disability benefits on a technicality?
- The disability application or "record" will be closed effective with the ALJ's decision, prohibiting U.S. District Courts from accepting or considering relevant and material evidence that might prove that the claimant is disabled. This likely will result in thousands of new disability claims each year in the form of re-applications. This subtle bureaucratic change realistically could result in the loss of significant retroactive benefits for those who refile with evidence of disability with an onset date within the scope of the previous application. There is no reason to close the record at any time other than to reduce the ability of claimants to present relevant evidence to support their claim. This will surely lead to decisions to deny benefits to claimants who are disabled under the law. Some of the adverse affects of this new closing of the record regulations are:
  - Loss of complete or partial coverage for Social Security Disability Insurance
  - Loss of coverage for Medicare benefits entirely
  - Loss of retroactive Medicaid and Medicare coverage for a period of time covered by current rules (from the date the claim was initially filed to the date of the subsequent application).

Such uncertainty regarding a key element of this change in the appellate process causes the Union to strongly suggest piloting any of these changes. Commissioner Barnhart has rejected pilots. Besides piloting the Reviewing Official step replacing the reconsideration, the Union feels that the Agency should pilot the decision to require that the reviewing official be an attorney. This decision ignores the fact that there are many highly qualified non-attorney employees in both SSA and the DDS's who are fully capable of deciding disability appeals and writing logical decisions. The Commissioner both insults the current workforce and creates difficult legal barriers for claimants to overcome in appeals. In an attorney dominated process (i.e., Reviewing Official and ALJ) claimants will almost be required to hire an attorney to manage their appeals at the earliest level. This adds an element of litigation that does not currently exist in the reconsideration appeal.

The Commissioner will replace the Appeals Council Review with a Decision Review Board (DRB). The DRB will be appointed by the Commissioner to review and correct ALJ decisions including approved claims. The DRB will not review decisions by state officials (DDSs) or Federal Reviewing Officials (FRO). This will prevent processing payment of an approved claim and will render the ALJs decision as not final. The process by which cases will be selected for review will be entirely at the DRB discretion and will provide the DRB with carte blanche authority to pick cases in a non-random manner. Such unregulated authority is an invitation for abuse

The Appeals Council currently either reverses or remands 30% of claims that they review.

Eliminating an appeal where such a large number of cases are either reversed or where all the evidence was not properly assessed insures that many claimants will be denied benefits that would be approved under the current system. Is this the desire of Congress? Does Congress really want to scale back the SSA disability program so that claimants approved under the current system are now denied benefits?

- A claimant's last appeal, U.S. District Court, requires legal representation. This will severely disadvantage claimants who lack the financial resources to either hire an attorney or travel to District Court. Additionally, the U.S. District Court system which is already overwhelmed is not prepared to absorb this influx of additional cases.

Commissioner Barnhart's new approach fails to address the problems and inadequacies of the State Disability Determination Services (DDS), which is responsible for the initial disability decision in all claims. AFGE strongly believes that if the initial claims level were addressed, the need for such drastic changes to the appeal levels would be unnecessary. But most of all, it would insure disabled claimants were paid much sooner.

There is no consistency in State DDS disability determinations. The taxpayer's chances of being approved for disability benefits continue to depend more on where they live and their income.

For example, State Agency Operations records indicate that those who can obtain medical attention early and often have a better chance of being approved for benefits than those who have a limited income or resources. (See Chart Below) Nationwide, those applying for Social Security disability have a much greater chance of being approved than those who may only apply for the Supplement Security Income (SSI) program. State Agency records clearly expose the inconsistencies of the State DDS decisions.

More than 66 percent of Social Security disability claims for benefits are approved in the Washington DC DDS, while only less than 28 percent of those who file for benefits are approved in the South Carolina DDS. Of those who applied for SSI benefits, the State of New Hampshire leads with more than a 59 percent allowance rate. However, residents from the States of Michigan, Ohio, Iowa and Georgia are approved less than 35 % of the time by their respective DDS. The concurrent disability process shows inexplicable variable allowance rates depending on the state of residence. Allowance rates are low in every state. The states of New Hampshire, Arizona and the District of Columbia approve more than 43 percent of the concurrent claims. Less than 18 percent of those filing concurrent disability claims are approved in Iowa, Missouri, and South Carolina.

As an illustration, following is a compilation of the allowance rates in a sample of states:

	T2		T16		Concurrent	
	Initial		Initial		Initial	
	Allow	Deny	Allow	Deny	Allow	Deny
NATIONAL AVERAGE	44.2	55.8	36.4	63.6	25.3	74.7
BOSTON Region	53.7	46.3	43.6	56.4	33	68
Boston, MA	56.9	43.1	48.7	51.3	36.6	63.4
New Hampshire	63.8	36.2	59.2	40.8	48.2	51.8
Connecticut	47.3	52.7	34.3	66.7	23.5	76.5
New York Region	51.4	48.6	42.8	57.2	33	67
Buffalo, NY	47	53	33.8	66.2	23	77
Newark, NJ	60.8	39.6	42.1	57.9	34.9	65.1
Puerto Rico	34.2	65.8	—	—	—	—
Philadelphia Region	51.7	48.3	40.3	59.7	28.9	71.1
Maryland	49.9	50.1	35.4	64.6	24.9	75.1
PA	53.3	46.7	41.8	58.2	28.1	71.9
WA, DC	66.1	33.9	54.8	45.2	45.5	54.5
Atlanta Region	34.9	65.1	30.1	69.9	21.2	78.8
Georgia	30.3	69.7	27.1	72.9	19.1	80.9
Kentucky	39.4	60.6	33.3	66.7	21.1	78.9
Birmingham	38.4	61.6	27.5	72.5	20.7	79.3
Florida	38.5	61.5	35.5	64.5	26.4	73.6
Miami	43.7	56.3	44.8	55.2	35.6	64.4
S. Carolina	28.2	71.8	26	74	17.7	82.3
Chicago Region	41.9	58.1	30.8	69.2	21.4	78.6
Illinois	43.8	56.2	30.4	69.6	23.9	76.1
Michigan	39.3	60.7	29.9	70.1	19.7	80.3
Detroit	32	68	26.4	73.6	16.5	83.5
Ohio	39.4	60.6	27.1	72.9	19.1	80.9
Wisconsin	46.9	53.1	34	66	21.4	78.6
Dallas Region	44.2	55.8	39.2	60.8	28.2	71.8
Texas	42.7	57.3	41.6	58.4	28.6	71.4
New Mexico	47	53	44.8	55.2	31.2	68.8
Oklahoma	43.1	56.7	36.8	63.2	24.4	75.6
Shreveport	53.8	46.2	37.3	62.7	35.3	64.7
Kansas City Region	43.6	56.4	30.5	69.5	17.9	82.1
Missouri	42.9	57.1	29.8	70.2	17.4	82.6
Iowa	45.5	54.5	32.3	67.7	16.4	83.6
Denver Region	38.5	61.5	39.1	60.9	21.5	78.5
Colorado	35	65	38.6	61.4	20.5	79.5
N. Dakota	51.2	48.8	39.6	60.4	28.1	71.9
S. Dakota	45.4	54.6	34.9	65.1	18.9	81.1
San Francisco Region	50.9	49.1	44.4	55.6	32.4	67.4
Arizona	59.3	40.7	51.8	48.2	43.3	56.7
California	50.8	49.2	43.9	56.1	31.8	68.2
Bay Area	60.6	39.4	52.5	47.5	36.6	63.4
L. A. East	49.4	50.6	49.8	50.2	37.4	92.5
L. A. West	54.4	45.6	49.6	50.4	34.5	65.5
Central Valley	48.1	51.9	39.3	60.7	28.2	71.8
Sacramento	54	46	38	62	29.7	70.3
Seattle Region	43.1	56.9	41.3	58.7	24.3	75.7
Oregon	35.4	64.6	34.7	65.3	18.8	81.2
Seattle	45.4	54.6	45.4	54.6	27.1	72.9

In a system where everyone is taxed equally, this is difficult to explain or justify. Claimants are entitled to quality consistent decisions not withstanding their state of residence or whether they are filing for Social Security or SSI disability benefits.

According to GAO,[1] a majority of DDSs do not conduct long-term, comprehensive workforce planning, which should include key strategies for recruiting, retaining, training and otherwise developing a workforce capable of meeting long term goals. The State DDS' lack uniform minimum qualifications for Disability Examiners (DE's) have high turnover rates for employees and do not provide ongoing training for DE's. This seems to be mostly attributed to low State employee pay and benefit scales and budget constraints.

[1] GAO–04–121

AFGE is convinced that SSA is not able or willing to correct these problems. AFGE has expressed these very concerns to the Subcommittee for several years and has seen little improvement with the State DDS situation. The State DDSs are required to use different rules that those at the hearing levels. This too has not changed with the Commissioner's new plan. This is a key problem that must be reconciled in order to reform the disability system. AFGE strongly believes that the only way to resolve the problems that plague the State DDSs is to federalize them. This will bring consistency to the initial claims decisions in the same way it resolved the Supplemental Security Income problems in 1974.

AFGE has recently become aware of the preliminary Systems Impact Assessment of SSA program modifications needed to accommodate the new disability determination process. The modifications considered necessary will be massive, leaving few programs untouched. Some of the systems changes will involve modifications to State DDS systems, which will have to be coordinated. SSA firewalls will require safeguarding and all software written for such modifications will require approval from the Architectural Review Board. However, approval is not certain and programs should require extensive testing before use.

AFGE finds the extent of these required modifications to be alarming. Is it reasonable, to begin implementation in the Boston Region before such systems changes can be made? SSA's budgets for FY06 and FY07 do not provide the money that will be needed to accomplish the systems changes necessary. Where do the resources come from to make these changes? If SSA devotes all or most of its systems budget and manpower to the Commissioner's disability initiate, won't that adversely impact on the Agency's other systems requirements?

With staffing cuts and heavy workloads that continue to rise, is it reasonable to use resources for an untested, unpiloted theory, rather than to provide staffing on the front lines to improve public service? AFGE believes the answer is clearly NO.

Commissioner Barnhart's approach fails to implement new communication or adjudicative techniques that either improve service to the disabled claimant or result in a more accurate or expeditious decision. More importantly, these changes will not protect the rights and interests of people with disabilities.

In Conclusion

AFGE strongly believes the full costs of implementing this initiative should be determined and submitted to Congress before implementation. Once costs can be determined, approved and appropriated, the DSI should be piloted. The effectiveness of this initiative should be thoroughly tracked and reviewed by SSA and Congress before any further implementation should take place. Piloting should include not only the DSI plan but also other proposed solutions to the disability benefits problem such as the DCM and AO initiatives. After appropriate pilots the Agency and Congress will be more equipped to select the best solution to the problem.

Additionally, AFGE strongly urges Congress to direct SSA to take corrective action with regards to the State DDS system and enact legislation which permits federal employees to make disability decisions without requiring the approval of the States.

Secondly, there will always be budget priorities. However, both workers and employers contribute to the Social Security system and are entitled to receive high quality service. It is entirely appropriate that spending for the administration of SSA programs be set at a level that fits the needs of Social Security's contributors and beneficiaries, rather than an arbitrary level that fits within the current political process.

In 2000, then Chairman Shaw and Rep. Benjamin Cardin reintroduced the Social Security Preparedness Act of 2000 (formerly H.R.5447), a bipartisan bill to prepare Social Security for the retiring baby boomers. AFGE strongly encourages this Subcommittee to reconsider introducing legislation that will provide SSA with the appropriate funding level to process all claims and all post-entitlement workloads timely.

Taking SSA's administrative expenses "off-budget" has vast support, not only from AFGE and SSA workers, but from senior and disability advocacy organizations. This would include AARP, the National Committee to Preserve Social Security and Medicare, the Alliance for Retired Americans, the Consortium for Citizens with Disabilities, and the Social Security Disability Coalition, just to name a few.

AFGE believes that by taking these costs OFF–BUDGET with the rest of the Social Security program, Social Security funds will be protected for the future and allow for new legislation, such as the Medicare Prescription Drug, Improvement, and Modernization Act of 2003 and the Intelligence Reform and Terrorism Prevention Act of 2004 to be implemented without comprising public service integrity. We believe this can be accomplished with strict congressional oversight to ensure the administrative resources are being spent efficiently.

AFGE is committed to serve as the employees' advocate and as a watchdog for clients, for taxpayers, and for their elected representatives.

Chairman MCCRERY. Mr. Hill.

STATEMENT OF JAMES A. HILL, PRESIDENT, CHAPTER 224, NATIONAL TREASURY EMPLOYEES UNION

Mr. HILL. Good afternoon, Chairman McCrery, Ranking Member Levin, and the Members of the Social Security Subcommittee.

My name is James Hill. I have worked as an attorney advisor in the Office of Disability Adjudication and Review (ODAR), formerly known as the Office of Hearing and Appeals for over 23 years.

I'm also the president of Chapter 224 of the National Treasury Employees Union that represents attorney advisors and other staff members in approximately 110 hearing offices and regional offices across the United States.

I thank the Subcommittee for inviting me to testify regarding the DSI initiative.

We now stand on a precipice of fundamental change. After an exhaustive review with input from many sources, Commissioner Barnhart formulated significant process changes that are set forth in the regulations that were issued on March 31, 2006. The planning stage is over. Now, implementation begins.

Commissioner Barnhart has proposed a lengthy and thoughtful implementation plan designed to identify and correct the inevitable unforeseen problems and to ensure DSI functions as expected.

The National Treasury Employees Union (NTEU) has consistently supported DSI, and we continue to do so.

Elements of the plan, such as the quick decision units, the elimination of the reconsideration determination, the creation of the FedRO position, the creation of medical vocational expert units, the elimination of the claimants' administrative appeal of ALJ decisions, the eventual elimination of the Appeals Council, the creation of the DRB, and the creation of an entirely new quality assurance process as presented in the regulations will significantly improve the disability adjudication process.

However, there are pitfalls that must be avoided if DSI is to succeed.

The quality assurance process must not stifle the ability of adjudicators and medical and vocational experts to exercise their independent judgment without undue influence.

The integrity of the FedRO decision must be maintained. It is essential that the FedRO decision not become merely another form of the discredited reconsideration determination.

We are also concerned that the locations of the FedROs and potentially poor working conditions will dissuade the best qualified candidates from applying for or accepting that position.

Finally, we are convinced that if the current backlog in hearing offices is not eliminated, it will strangle DSI. Simply put, if DSI must contend with backlogs as large as those that exist today, it will fail.

Currently, there are approximately 727,000 cases pending at ODAR hearing offices, and average processing time is nearly 480 days. Ideally, hearing offices should have no more than 350,000 cases.

Resources are tight, so any initiative designed to attack the backlog problem must do so without demanding a significant expenditure of resources.

Fortunately, history provides the vehicle for the resolution of the backlog problem: the Senior Attorney Program 1995 that produced over 220,000 fully favorable on the record decisions and was a key factor in reducing the cases pending in the late nineties from 550,000 to 311,000. This was accomplished with a modest expenditure of resources.

Unfortunately that program was terminated as part of the Hearings Process Improvement initiative.

We recommend that SSA reissue the regulations authorizing ODARs attorney advisors to issue fully favorable on the record decisions.

Properly administered, such a program could produce over 350,000 fully favorable on the record decisions over the next 4 years, reducing the number of cases pending to a workable level and requiring only a relative mild expenditure of resources.

I reiterate the support of NTEU for the DSI initiative.

Mr. Chairman, again, I appreciate the opportunity to testify before this Committee and would be happy to answer any questions Members of the Committee may have.

Thank you.

[The prepared statement of Mr. Hill follows:]

Statement of James Hill, President, Chapter 224, National Treasury Employees Union, Cleveland, Ohio

Good morning Chairman McCrery, Ranking Member Levin and members of the Subcommittee on Social Security. My name is James Hill. I have worked as an Attorney-Adviser in the Office of Disability Adjudication and Review (formerly the Office of Hearings and Appeals) for over 23 years. I am also the President of Chapter 224 of the National Treasury Employees Union (NTEU) that represents Attorney-Advisers and other staff members in approximately 110 Office of Disability Adjudication and Review (ODAR) Hearing and Regional Offices across the United States. I thank the Subcommittee for inviting me to testify regarding Commissioner Barnhart's proposal now known as the Disability Service Improvement Initiative (DSI) to reform the disability determination process. My testimony today represents the views of NTEU.

Since the early 1990's SSA hearing offices have been under severe stress caused by an adjudication process woefully inadequate to process the massive numbers of appeals of State Agency determinations. Cases pending at OHA hearing offices rose from approximately 180,000 in 1991 to approximately 550,000 cases nationwide by mid-1995. At that time SSA began the Senior Attorney Program which during its pendency from 1995 to early 2000 produced over 220,000 fully favorable on-the-record decisions. The number of cases pending at hearing offices was reduced to approximately 311,000 in September 1999. However, since 1999, a number of factors including the termination of the Senior Attorney Program, increased receipts, and the implementation of the disastrous Hearings Process Improvement Plan (HPI) have resulted in a record number of cases pending. Currently, there are approximately 727,000 cases pending at ODAR hearing offices with an average processing time of nearly 480 days. In some hearing offices processing time is approaching two years. All agree that this is not an acceptable level of service.

The current backlog was accumulated over the course of several years. Elimination of the backlog will take several years; there are no practical "quick fixes". Commissioner Barnhart recognized this fact and after a comprehensive and lengthy review of the current adjudication process, she proposed a number of fundamental changes. The changes in the disability process were codified in the final regulations published on March 31, 2006. The process by which these regulations were promulgated was lengthy and involved substantial interaction with entities internal and external to SSA that are interested in the disability process.

The final regulations significantly alter the disability adjudication process. They create a "quick decision process" to adjudicate those claimants who are obviously disabled. They eliminate the reconsideration determination and create an entirely new level of decision maker; the Federal Reviewing Official. The final regulations replace the Appeals Council with a Decision Review Board and indicate that an entirely new quality assurance system will be created that will function at each level of the process. The final regulations introduce a limited number of changes in the Administrative Law Judge hearing process but do not alter the essential nature of that process.

To facilitate the new disability adjudication process, Commissioner Barnhart has instituted organizational changes designed to facilitate the implementation of DSI. These changes include the creation of Quick Decision Units at the state agencies, the creation of the Office of Disability Adjudication and Review, and the creation of Medical and Vocational Expert Units. The components of the Office of Disability Adjudication and Review include the Office of the Chief Administrative Law Judge that oversees the operations of the Agency's hearing offices, the Office of the Chief Federal Reviewing Official that oversees the operations involving the Federal Reviewing Officials (FedRO), the Office of Appellate Operations (the Appeals Council) and the Office of the Decision Review Board.

Implementation of DSI will commence in the Boston Region on August 1, 2006. The Commissioner has wisely selected the Boston Region as the first to implement DSI for a number of reasons including its small size (currently the Boston Region has about 3% of the hearing office caseload) and state agencies that are efficiently processing their workloads. Notably, the Boston Region hearing offices are not troubled by the huge backlogs that afflict so many hearing offices across the United States. The Commissioner also has decided that DSI will not be expanded to other regions for at least a year. This permits the fine tuning that will certainly be necessary in order to achieve maximum efficiency. Only after DSI has proven its viability will it be expanded and even then, to other small regions initially.

Quick Decisions

In order to provide timely benefits to those who are "obviously disabled", the new regulations contain provisions for a "Quick Decision Process". This will significantly improve the disability adjudication process for those claimants with specified medical conditions that normally result in a finding of disability. The Commissioner projects that approximately 10% of initial claims can be handled through this process. While originally scheduled to be attached to various regional offices, the final regulation places these units in the various state agencies. This is an example of the flexibility shown by the Commissioner during the course of the comment period.

The Role of the Federal Reviewing Official (FedRO)

Perhaps the most innovative initiative contained in the regulations is the elimination of the reconsideration determination and the creation of the Federal Reviewing Official (FedRO) position, a federal attorney with complete adjudicatory authority that is placed between the State Agency and the Administrative Law Judge. It is absolutely essential that the FedRO process be more than a replacement for the current reconsideration determination which has very little credibility with the public or with ALJs.

If DSI is to fully succeed, the FedRO must introduce an element of credibility in disability adjudications prior to the ALJ hearing that is presently lacking. Currently, the State Agencies provide almost no rationale for their unfavorable determinations which seriously undermines their credibility. It is essential that the decisions made by the FedRO be recognized as independent decisions by an individual who has the discretion to award or deny benefits as justified by the record. The importance of attaining this credibility cannot be overstated. The final regulations removed some, but not all, of the ambiguity in the proposed regulations that led many to question whether the FedRO is an independent decision maker. If the FedRO turns out to be "just a federal reconsideration determination" DSI will fail.

To enhance the credibility of the FedRO decision, it must be a well reasoned, comprehensive and literate explanation of why a claimant is, or is not, entitled to disability benefits. To be effective the FedRO process must establish its credibility with claimants, the State Agencies, Administrative Law Judges and most importantly with the American public. This requires the legal expertise of an attorney to apply the rules, regulations and law to the evidence and to make and issue a legally defensible written decision. It also demands extensive knowledge and experience in evaluating the functional effects of medical impairments. The FedRO must have extensive legal and disability program knowledge and experience. Fortunately, SSA already employs personnel with the education, training, and experience to decide and draft disability decisions necessary to assure the success of the FedRO process—ODAR Attorney Advisers.

The expertise of each individual FedRO is vital to the success of DSI. It is essential that the Agency secure the best available applicants. The first 70 FedROs will be located in the Washington metropolitan area, close to or at ODAR headquarters. Given the number of unknown factors associated with the "start-up" of this new process, it is prudent that it be located centrally. However, there is a significant downside to such a centralized location in that many of the best qualified potential applicants will not compete for the positions simply because of the location and the general unattractiveness of the proposed working conditions. It is essential for the success of DSI that the key position in DSI, the FedRO, is accessible to those most qualified to successfully perform the requirement of the position. That entails locations convenient to those highly qualified individuals as well as working conditions conducive to enticing the best to apply and accept the appointment. Hopefully, SSA will recognize that acquiring the best possible applicants requires that the position must be made attractive, and in the future, it will adjust its hiring strategies to facilitate acquiring the best possible personnel.

There is a larger issue involved in the eventual placement of FedRO personnel. When citizens think about the Social Security Administration, they do not perceive it as a far off governmental bureaucracy located in Baltimore. Most do not even know that SSA headquarters is in Baltimore. When most citizens think of SSA, they do so in terms of their local SSA office where they can deal face to face with SSA employees who are their neighbors. This is an invaluable asset not only to SSA but to the public we serve. Is it likely that SSA would have delivered such spectacular service to the people of hurricane damaged Louisiana, Mississippi, Alabama, and Texas if it had been a faceless bureaucracy located somewhere inside the "Beltway"? SSA is what it is in part because it is neighbors serving their neighbors. The rationale that applies to the wisdom of maintaining local field and hearing offices should also apply to the FedRO. Citizens are much more comfortable dealing with their government on a local basis with people who are their neighbors, not strangers half a country away.

An important objective of DSI is to facilitate consistency at all decisional levels. The inconsistency of decision-making between the state agencies themselves, state agencies and ALJs, and even among ALJs themselves has been a constant source of criticism. However, it must be understood and accepted, that the complexity of disability determinations and the difference in the effects of medical conditions on each individual leads to some perceived inconsistency in the decisional results. Nonetheless, the final regulations do facilitate decisional consistency without interfering with the decisional independence of adjudicators at all three levels through several modalities including the FedRO process itself and a comprehensive quality assurance program.

The requirement that the FedRO produce a well reasoned legally defensible decision using the same rulings, regulations, court decisions, and statutes as are used by the ALJ should greatly enhance decisional consistency. DSI initiates feedback loops among the various levels of adjudication that will provide each level with insight into the thought processes of the other decision makers. If the FedRO decision is different from that of the State Agency, the FedRO's written decision will explain to the State Agency why a different decision was reached. This level of communication, both formal and informal, between the FedRO and State Agency will result in improved decision making by both entities and promote decisional consistency without adversely affecting the claimants.

The increased level of decisional consistency promoted by the regulations will result in the reality and the perception that the proper decision is being made at the earliest possible time. The FedRO decision will present the ALJ and the claimant with a comprehensive explanation of why the Agency denied the claim. While it imposes no limitation on the ALJ, it does help focus the issues in controversy leading to a more efficient hearing process. By providing the claimant with a detailed explanation of why his/her application was denied, the FedRO assists the claimant and his/her representative in marshalling evidence needed to establish disability.

The ALJ Hearing

The final regulations wisely retain the Administrative Law Judge hearing process essentially unchanged. Hearing offices will continue to prepare cases for hearing, Administrative Law Judges will continue to conduct due process hearings, and the decisional independence of the ALJ continues to be protected by the APA. However, concern had been expressed about the relationship between the FedRO and the ALJ. The final regulations make it clear that the FedRO decision is not entitled to any deference on the part of the ALJ. The Commissioner's Plan recognizes that the reality of the *de novo* hearing must be maintained and the freedom of the ALJ to decide cases based upon his/her evaluation of the evidence and the appropriate law and regulations must be preserved.

Elimination of the Appeals Council

Another bold initiative of DSI is the elimination of the Appeals Council and the claimant's right to make an administrative appeal of the ALJ decision. While on its surface the elimination of the Appeals Council appears to be detrimental to claimants, that is not the case. The effect of the elimination of the Appeals Council must not be viewed in isolation, but in the context of the entire adjudicatory process. Improvements in the decision making process at the State Agency level, the introduction of the RO, and the quality assurance program proposed by the Commissioner render the administrative review of ALJ decisions unnecessary. We believe that considering the Commissioner's New Approach in its totality, an additional administrative appeal of the ALJ decision is unnecessary.

As currently constituted the Appeals Council serves two distinct purposes. It serves as an appellate body and as a quality assurance entity, but performs neither with distinction. This is not intended to disparage the hard-working employees at the Appeals Council, but rather its basic concept and design. The final regulations replace the Appeals Council with an end-of-line review by a centralized quality control unit known as the Decision Review Board. The Agency, in its effort to improve quality assurance at the ALJ level of adjudication, should take care not to repeat its mistakes of the early 1980s when it attempted to interfere with ALJ decisional independence. The final regulations recognize that in order to avoid the appearance of interference with ALJ decisional independence, it is essential that ALJs be intimately involved in any quality assurance program.

There is concern that the lack of a right of administrative appeal of the decisions of Administrative Law Judges will result in a substantial increase in the caseload of the District Courts. We agree that any action that significantly increases the caseload of the district courts is unacceptable. However, we believe that the assumption that eliminating the Appeals Council will significantly increase District Court caseload is unwarranted. While such an assumption is sustainable if one considers the elimination of the Appeals Council in isolation, it is far less sustainable when one considers the whole breadth of the Commissioner's plan. In that light, we expect that after a period of adjustment, the increased quality of the adjudication system will actually decrease the number of cases filed at the District Court. It will certainly significantly decrease the number of voluntary remands. In any event, the measured implementation process that limits DSI to the Boston Region for at least one year will permit an opportunity to observe the impact of the elimination of the Appeals Council on the number of court filings.

While appealing unfavorable ALJ decisions directly to the District Court is appropriate, claimants should not have to file an action in the District Court to contest a dismissal of a Request for Hearing. The final regulations permit claimants to appeal dismissals to the Disability Review Board.

AeDIB

The Commissioner has made it clear that inauguration of her new approach is predicated upon the successful implementation of AeDIB. SSA has had sufficient experience with implementing substantial process changes without ensuring the necessary system improvements are in place to know the dangers of premature implementation. Fortunately, AeDIB is progressing as well as can be expected. Components of AeDIB such as digital recording of hearings, video teleconferencing for conducting hearings, and a new case management system (CPMS) have been successfully accomplished. Decision writing templates that significantly improve the quality of written ALJ decisions have been enthusiastically received and continue to be made even more user friendly. The Agency has determined that dual monitors are necessary to maximize the utility of the electronic folder and in fact has commenced the purchase and distribution of a second monitor to those employees who duties require the use of two monitors. Of course the most important and most complex component of AeDIB is the electronic folder itself.

The savings, both in time and money, that will be realized by converting from paper folders to electronic folders are substantial and will result in improved service to the public. The electronic folder will significantly increase the Agency's flexibility in managing its workload and permit cases to be processed more expeditiously. Implementing electronic folders is a massive undertaking and the consequences of failure are catastrophic. However, the realistic attitude and the competency of Agency personnel charged with the responsibility of implementing the electronic folder has resulted in a process that is proceeding as well as can be expected. They have demonstrated a capacity to listen to the comments from end users and introduce improvements on a nearly continual basis. There is every reason to expect the electronic folder to be a technical success. However, the Agency should recognize that the fundamental differences in the interface between employees and the electronic folder and the current interface between employees and paper folders may render some tasks more time consuming than is presently the case.

The Backlog at Hearing Offices

The disability backlog problem at ODAR is neither recent nor entirely intractable, but it is persistent.

Cases Pending at ODAR Hearing Offices

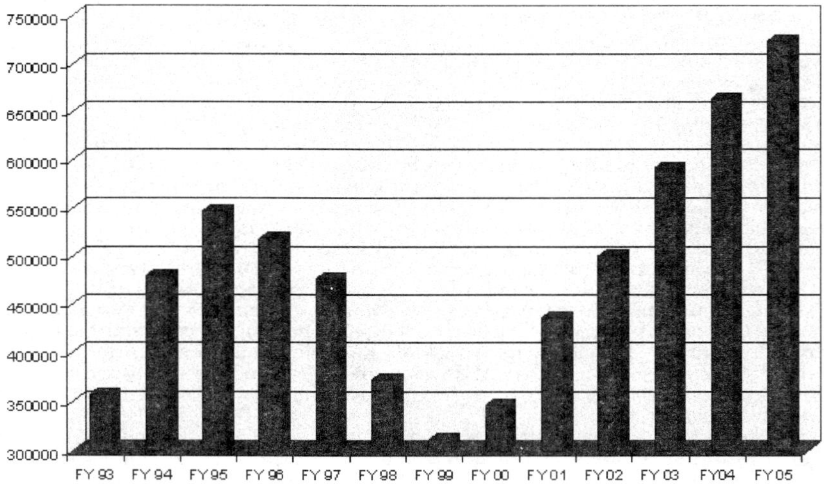

As of the end of April 2006 there were 727,629 cases pending at ODAR hearing offices. The optimal level of cases for efficient ODAR HO operations is 350,000 cases. While DSI will significantly improve the adjudication process, it will have little impact on the current backlog. In fact, if the backlog problem is not addressed it will strangle the Commissioner's DSI initiative. Unless the backlog at ODAR hearing offices is eliminated, DSI will be no more effective in providing timely service they we are now. Fortunately, history provides the vehicle for the resolution of the backlog problem—the Senior Attorney Program begun in 1995. The solution is to use current staff to perform the adjudication needed to deal with this problem.

It is not a coincidence that during the time the Senior Attorney Program was in operation (1995–2000) the number of cases pending at OHA hearing offices declined, nor is it a coincidence that the number of cases pending increased after the Senior Attorney Program was terminated as part of the Hearings Process Improvement Plan (HPI). Over its five year history, the Senior Attorney Program produced 220,000 decisions which when combined with record ALJ productivity reduced the number of cases pending at hearing offices from 550,000 to 311,000 cases. This was accomplished with a relatively modest expenditure of resources. HPI eliminated the Senior Attorney Program because it was believed that the Senior Attorney Program was no longer necessary. The termination of the Senior Attorney Program, the implementation of the disastrous HPI initiative and increased receipts have resulted in a record number of cases pending. ODAR has a serious backlog problem, and there is no reason to expect a significant improvement in the foreseeable future.

As discouraging as the increase of cases pending may be, it does not fully reflect the harmful effect of the backlog on the public. Average processing time at the hearing office level was approximately 270 days at the beginning of FY 2000; now it is nearly 480 days. In some locales, claimants have to wait nearly two years for a hearing. This is an unconscionably long wait for a disability decision, and it is causing untold harm to some of the most vulnerable members of society. None will dispute that the public deserves far better service than SSA is presently providing.

The backlog has risen despite system and process improvements and record ALJ productivity levels. Current initiatives have not materially affected the backlog because they fail to deal with the underlying causes of the backlog. The root causes of the hearing office backlog are the number of receipts, too few adjudicators for the size of the caseload, and an inefficient adjudicatory process. Little can be done about the number of receipts. Fiscal considerations preclude acquiring the massive number of ALJs that would be required to effectively reduce the backlog. ODAR must look elsewhere for the additional adjudicators temporarily needed to deal with the backlog problem.

Consistent with my testimony at previous hearings, we recommend implementing an improved Senior Attorney Adjudicator Program. If implemented this program would produce approximately 370,000 high quality favorable decisions over the next four fiscal years, effectively eliminating the backlog by the end of FY 2010, with a minimal increase in resources. Additionally, none of those cases would need to be worked up (pulled) as Senior Attorney Adjudicators would review and decide unpulled cases. This will significantly reduce the backlog of cases to be pulled.

A Senior Attorney Adjudicator Program would invest the authority to issue fully favorable on-the-record (OTR) decisions in all hearing level attorneys with at least 3 years experience. All qualified ODAR attorneys with at least three years' experience would assume decision making as well as ALJ decision drafting duties. The addition of decision making duties necessarily reduces decision writing capacity. However, because most ALJ decision writing will continue to be done by attorneys, replacing lost decision writing capacity can be accomplished by redirecting current assets. The original Senior Attorney Program demonstrated the validity of this concept. To further ensure quality, all Senior Attorney decisions would be drafted in the new decisional templates, formatted for Senior Attorney signature, and a Lead Senior Attorney position would be created. This individual would review hearing office (HO) decision drafts, including those drafted by Senior Attorneys, and provide feedback on quality to management, the writers and the Senior Attorneys.

The large number of Senior Attorneys who would perform both the function of decision maker and decision writer ensures that each hearing office would have maximum flexibility in managing its workload. Requiring that Senior Attorneys still draft ALJ decisions ensures that ALJs continue to have access to the most skilled and experienced decision writers. No DSI cases would be subject to adjudication by a Senior Attorney.

In addition to making a positive, immediate, and effective impact on the backlog, a Senior Attorney Adjudicator Program would act as a training program for the Federal Reviewing Official (FedRO) position. Over the next five years, SSA will hire or promote over 2000 attorneys for the FedRO position that the Commissioner has repeatedly declared to be the linchpin of DSI. Hiring new attorneys in ODAR hearing offices will permit them to learn the SSA disability adjudication process under the mentorship of Senior Attorneys and Administrative Law Judges. Eventually, those successful as Attorney Advisers would become Senior Attorneys. Those successful as Senior Attorneys would be prime candidates for the FedRO position. The selection of FedROs would be based on demonstrated performance and not the vagaries of a merit selection system.

The conversion of a large number of ODAR Attorney Advisers to part time decision making Senior Attorneys will result in an immediate and substantial improvement in ODAR service to the public at minimal additional cost. Based upon the Agency's experience with the original Senior Attorney Program, and with the full cooperation of hearing office management (lacking during the original Senior Attorney Program), this initiative could produce as many as 100,000 quality decisions a year without diminishing ALJ productivity or changing the overall payment rate. Based upon previous experience, the average processing time for these cases would be approximately 100 days. Additionally, the minimal staff time and complete lack of ALJ time spent on these cases frees the staff and ALJs to spend more time on processing those cases requiring a hearing. The staff will benefit greatly from the significant reduction in the pulling workload caused by the Senior Attorney Adjudicator Program. The reduction of the backlog will significantly enhance the ability of hearing offices to more efficiently transition from paper to electronic files and will enable hearing offices to effectively fulfill their role in the DSI process.

The savings in administrative costs to the Agency and human costs to the claimants by eliminating unnecessary hearings would be substantial. Adjudicating cases that should have been paid without the need for ALJ involvement will not only provide much more timely service to those disabled claimants, but it will free ALJs to hear only those cases requiring a hearing thereby shortening the time those claimants must wait for a disability decision. The savings and improved service that would result from the implementation of a Senior Attorney Adjudicator Program based upon the original Senior Attorney Program would be substantial. This program would greatly facilitate the transition from the current system to DSI.

Mr. Chairman, again, I appreciate the opportunity to testify before this committee and would be happy to answer any questions members of the committee may have. Thank you.

Chairman MCCRERY. Thank you, Mr. Hill. Judge Bernoski.

STATEMENT OF THE HONORABLE RONALD G. BERNOSKI, PRESIDENT, ASSOCIATION OF ADMINISTRATIVE LAW JUDGES

Mr. BERNOSKI. Thank you. Thank you, Mr. Chairman. Thank you for inviting us to testify here today.

I appear as the president of the Association of ALJs, and we represent about 1,100 ALJs in the SSA, and there are about 1,400 ALJs in the entire Federal government.

We support the commissioner's plan for reform of the Social Security disability process, and we worked with her during the development of the plan, and we've committed to work with her during its startup in Region I and its rollout across the country.

However, in our opinion, the changes in the plan cannot occur without help from outside sources, and the major support must come from Congress, because the plan must be properly funded. The failure to fund the changes will lead to failure of the plan and to catastrophic results, including unprecedented backlogs, all to the harm of the American people.

Now, with regard to particular aspects of the plan, the reviewing official, or the FedRO, will require new funding, and this change, as indicated previously today, is really, and we agree, the centerpiece of the reform plan.

The primary function of the FedRO is to ensure that the cases are completely prepared for hearing and to award cases that meet the standard for disability as early possible in the process.

Now, we all know that it takes time to prepare a case for trial and it is vital that SSA does not expect these FedROs to do too much.

Now, we have heard that the FedROs will be expected to produce two cases per day. However, we believe that this is more than a person can accomplish while producing a quality work product.

The expectation of two cases per day was one of the reasons that caused the Adjudication Officer (AO) program to fail, and we should learn from that failure not to commit the same mistake again.

Requiring too much from the FedRO will result in poorly developed case files and the wrong cases being paid. If ALJs receive poorly developed files, we'll have the same amount of work as we do now, but we'll have fewer support staff to assist us, which is going to lead to larger backlogs.

We are of the opinion that at least two FedROs plus support staff will be required for each ALJ.

Now, the plan requires that the FedRO position be staffed by an attorney, and we are of the opinion that the skill and training of an attorney is vital to perform the responsibilities of this position and to producing the expected quality of work product.

Now, also, the separation between the ALJ and the FedRO must be maintained. It must be remembered that the ALJ does not hear the case on appeal from the FedRO, but instead conducts a de novo hearing.

The ALJs are required to make decisions based on the evidence that was produced at the hearing and for the record, and judges should not be expected to comment on the differing aspects of the FedRO determination, because this only creates an opportunity to claim error on appeal.

We further believe that the ALJ hearing must become more structured under the reform plan.

Our cases will now go directly to the Federal courts, go the Federal courts on appeal, and the courts are going to require a higher quality work product. This will require more sophisticated medical and vocational expert testimony be produced at our hearings, and that better written hearing decisions be prepared by attorney writers.

It is of little value for us to conduct an excellent hearing if the work product does not capture it in a well-written and analyzed decision.

Now, in closing, Mr. Chairman, the commissioner should be given credit for assuming the huge task of converting our paper file system to the electronic eDib system, but again, this program is going to have to be fully funded.

Experience has shown at least initially that the conversion from the electronic file to the eDib—or from the paper to the eDib system has slowed down the processing time, and our judges have reported to us that the electronic system itself is slow, and this is reducing the amount of work that the user can produce; and both of these factors are going to reduce the number of cases that can be heard and the number of decisions that can be written, and funds must be provided to correct this problem within the system.

Now, in closing, SSA is the only adjudicative body that not have established rules of procedure, and we believe that comprehensive rules must be adopted to provide the structure that's needed to implement this new process.

Thank you very much.

[The prepared statement of Mr. Bernoski follows:]

Statement of Judge Ronald G. Bernoski, President, Association of Administrative Law Judges, Inc., Sussex, Wisconsin

Mr. Chairman and Members of the Subcommittee:

I. INTRODUCTION

Thank you for the opportunity to testify before you today. My name is Ronald G. Bernoski. I am an Administrative Law Judge ("ALJ") who has been hearing Social Security disability cases at the Office of Disability Adjudication and Review (ODAR) of the Social Security Administration ("SSA") in Milwaukee, Wisconsin, for over 25 years.

I am the President of the Association of Administrative Law Judges ("AALJ"). Our organization represents the administrative law judges employed in the Social Security Administration and the Department of Health and Human Services ("DHHS"). One of the stated purposes of the AALJ is to promote and preserve full due process hearings in compliance with the Administrative Procedure Act for those individuals who seek adjudication of program entitlement disputes within the SSA. The AALJ represents about 1100 of the approximate 1400 administrative law judges in the Federal government.

I. STATEMENT

The Association of Administrative Law Judges supports the Commissioner's reform plan for the Social Security disability system. We have endorsed the plan and we have worked with Deputy Commissioner Martin Gerry to improve it during the developmental phase of the plan. As a result, some of our proposals have been included in the final regulations. We have an agreement with the Commissioner to work closely with her during the implementation of the reform plan which will begin in Region I. We have both made a commitment to have frequent meetings during this initial phase to look for problems areas and to ensure success of the "start-up". We will continue to work, in a like manner, with Deputy Commissioner Lisa de Soto (ODAR) to achieve success as the plan starts in Region I and expands across the nation.

However, we believe that the changes included in the reform of the Social Security disability system can not occur in a vacuum, and that assistance will be required from outside sources. The major outside support must come from Congress as the reform plan must be fully funded. The failure to completely fund the changes will lead to catastrophic results including unprecedented backlogs. As a result, the American people will suffer by having to wait even longer for their critically important hearings.

Federal Reviewing Official

The Federal Reviewing Official (FRO) will require new funding. We agree with the Commissioner that the FRO is the "center piece" of the reform and if it fails the entire reform plan will fail. We are of the opinion that at least two FRO's, plus support staff, will be required for each administrative law judge (judge). The primary function of the FRO is to ensure that cases will be completely developed and ready for hearing. The FRO will have the further responsibility to identify the claims that meet the standards for SSA disability and award those claims as early as possible in the process. This function is an extremely time consuming task, because it requires the FRO to work closely with both physicians and attorneys in the preparing the hearing files. Physicians and attorneys are both extremely busy professionals and frequently multiple contacts are needed to obtain requested information. As we all know, it takes time to prepare a case for trial. It will be a serious error to place an unreasonable production requirement on the FRO's. The production number which has been whispered in the halls of ODAR of two fully developed cases per day will ultimately result in poor quality work and remands back to the FRO from the judge. In our view, a production requirement of this level could not be met under normal sustained working condition and would not yield the quality work product expected and needed from the FRO's. We must remember that the high production requirement of two cases per day, was one of the major factors leading to the failure of the piloted Adjudication Officer program in the 1990's. The Adjudication Officer had many of the same functions and responsibilities of the FRO and we should acknowledge the reasons for the failure of that program and learn from our past mistakes. If the FRO fails to perform as expected, the judges will receive poorly developed case files. This failure will leave us in a worse condition than we now experience. The reform plan anticipates that judges will have fewer support staff. If a failure in the reform results in the same workload for the judges, and we have fewer support staff, we will never be able to hear and decide our cases in a timely and high quality manner. The result will be an increase in the case backlog which will be to the detriment of the American people. High production requirements for the FRO also carry with it the potential of resulting in too many claims being awarded or the wrong claims being paid. We are certain that this is not the result intended by the Commissioner in developing this reform plan.

Attorneys as FRO's

The reform plan requires that the FRO position will be staffed by persons who are trained as attorneys. We are of the opinion that this is a vital component of the plan. The skill and training of an attorney is needed to adequately perform the responsibilities of this position. An attorney is best qualified to provide high quality legal analysis and legal writing required to completely perform the responsibilities of this position, as well as similar positions in the hearing office.

Interaction Between the Judges and FRO

As stated above, the primary responsibility of the FRO is to develop the evidence in the case and prepare the case for hearing. The judges must receive a complete work product from the FRO for the new process to be a success. When preparing the written hearing decision the judge should not be required to comment on elements in the decision of the FRO that differ from the decision of the judge. The case is not before the judge on appeal from the FRO. Instead, the judge conducts a *de novo* hearing on the claim and makes a finding based on the evidence produced for the record during a face-to-face hearing. In fact, this is the only time in the entire SSA disability process (including Federal court) where the claimant is given an opportunity to appear and "state his/her case" to a government official. It is thereby vital that the decision be based on the evidence in the hearing record with the judge weighing the evidence and making credibility findings. This decision should not be encumbered by requiring comments on the FRO decision, which are not relevant to the hearing evidence. Any required commenting only provides an opportunity to claim error on appeal.

The Administrative Law Judge Hearing

We are of the opinion that the administrative law judge hearing must become more structured and formal in the new process. This will require that more sophisticated medical and vocational expert witness testimony be produced at the hearing and that a well written decision be prepared by the decision writer. The most frequent complaint that we hear from the judges, and the United States District courts, relates to the poor decisional quality. Regrettably, this result obtains in many cases because of the poor quality of the writing from our non-legal writing staff who, for the most part, have no formal education beyond high school. It is of little value for the judge to conduct an excellent hearing with sophisticated evidence if the same is not captured and correctly analyzed in the written hearing decision. In administrative law, the written decision remains a vital part of the case record, and the most common criticism we receive from the Federal courts relates to the lack of an adequate rationale in our decisions. Since under the new process, most of our cases will go directly to the Federal courts on appeal we will be required to perform at a level expected by the Federal courts. If we do not meet this expectation, the agency will receive severe criticism from the courts and will suffer lasting embarrassment. A significant part of this problem can be addressed by requiring that all decision writers be trained as attorneys, but the hearing process must also be improved. Writing templates which have been developed by the agency could never substitute for the training and education received by attorneys. Legal training equips them with the necessary tools to correctly analyze and write legally defensible decisions.

The Electronic File, e-DIB

The Commissioner should be given credit for her leadership in converting the SSA paper file system to an electronic process. This has been a large undertaking and it moves SSA into a modern system of record keeping. e-DIB, or the electronic file, must also be fully funded both for its implementation and subsequent needed improvements. Funds must be available to provide sufficient electronic equipment for the judges, staff, hearing rooms, claimant use and remote hearing sites. Hearing rooms must also be increased in size to allow space for the installation of the new electronic equipment. The hearing rooms must be designed for safety with measures taken to "build in" or conceal the numerous wires that are now lying on the floors in the currently retrofitted hearing rooms. The current retrofitted undersized hearing rooms, with wires lying about, create a dangerous environment for both claimants and SSA employees.

Experience with e-DIB has shown that use of the electronic file slows the work process at all levels, including both the DDS and administrative law judge levels. We have also received information from our judges indicating that the current e-DIB system reacts very slowly to user commands. This poor response time slows down the user of the equipment and reduces the amount of work that can be produced. The result of both factors will be an increase in the case backlog because fewer cases will be heard and fewer decisions will be written. We have discussed this problem with agency officials, and they have assured us that they are aware of this problem and are working to have it corrected. We are of the opinion that funding must be provided to correct this soft ware problem and to increase the speed of the e-DIB system.

Rules of Procedures

We are the only adjudicative body in this country that does not have established rules of procedure. About five years ago the agency and the AALJ formed a Joint Rules Committee to developed proposed rules of procedure. The Committee worked for several years developing an excellent proposed code consisting of rules of procedure that were in a large part based on the existing rules of the Department of

Labor. The proposed rules were given to the Commissioner and she incorporated some of the rules into the new process, but many have not been implemented.

We are of the opinion that the remaining rules should be implemented by the agency. These are not substantive rules and do not require "notice and comment" under the Administrative Procedure Act. Since most SSA claimants are represented, these rules are needed to provide structure to our hearing system. The rules can provide for a relaxing of the procedural rules for *pro* se claimants.

The proposed rules will are provide the formality and structure required by the Federal courts. We have pledged to work with the Commissioner on developing these rules, and we are of the opinion that it will be a serious error not to promulgate these rules.

Chairman MCCRERY. Mr. Flack.

STATEMENT OF GARY FLACK, CHAIRMAN, SOCIAL SECURITY SECTION, FEDERAL BAR ASSOCIATION

Mr. FLACK. Mr. Chairman, the Social Security section of the Federal Bar Association (FBA) welcomes this opportunity to share our thoughts about the new final regulations to improve the disability claims process.

I am the Chair of the Social Security section of the FBA.

We commend Commissioner Barnhart for her efforts to improve the disability determination process. This Subcommittee is also to be congratulated for its oversight role in having conducted hearings on the problem and now on the solution.

Today I focus my testimony on several aspects of the final rule.

First, will the reviewing official delay proceedings or become an institutional hurdle claimants must overcome?

The office of the FedRO is a more accessible but federally controlled decisionmaker. Unless there are at least as many FedROs as ALJs, the caseload of each FedRO will soon exceed the heavy caseload that the ALJs have today.

Too large a caseload will not only delay decisionmaking but also interfere with accurate decisionmaking, so we agree with the others that there have got to be plenty of FedROs.

Also, we're concerned that the FedRO decisions may become an institutional barrier in disability determinations.

Some ALJs may utilize the FedRO decision to deny benefits. Other ALJs may regard it as a hurdle the claimant must overcome.

If an ALJ reverses the FedRO's decision, then the DRB may question the ALJ's decision based on the earlier FedRO decision.

The commissioner must provide procedural guarantees to assure the independence of the ALJ's decisionmaking. It is the fair hearing that's the centerpiece of the disability adjudication process, not the FedRO.

Our second concern is how the Federal judiciary is used as a measure of the success of the DSI. This has been addressed by several of the speakers, and the commissioner as well.

We think that it's great that the commissioner is developing all these different statistics as to whether there's a voluntary remand, whether there are substantive mistakes, and looking at these numbers is critical to accurately see how the program is working.

One thing that I don't think many speakers have mentioned is that you have to keep track of Sentence 6 remands when there's new and material evidence that somehow didn't get into the system before. If there's a lot of those Sentence 6 remands, then the system isn't working as well as it should.

Our third concern is will Region I predict how well DSI will work elsewhere?

The appendices attached to our written testimony suggest that Region I, as you noted, is already approving an above average number of claims with very few court challenges. The system is working pretty well there.

We conclude that the pilot project may work well in Region I, but poorly elsewhere.

As we noted in our materials, it's likely to take about 3 years before you get accurate numbers from the district court, because it takes a long time for all this to play out, so we're not sure how quickly this system can be rolled out.

Our final concern is whether the DRB will undermine the independence of the ALJs.

We fear that the DRB and its computer-based predictive model will intrude on the traditional independence of ALJs.

The ALJs worry that the benefits of a fair hearing will be overturned by a review board that did not see the claimant or attend the hearing.

Private practitioners worry that the computer program, not the individual ALJ, will become the de facto decisionmaker.

The commissioner's computer-based predictive model probably will not be as blunt as the discredited Bellmon review, but we fear it will unduly shape ALJ decisions.

Thank you for the opportunity to appear before you today. I'd be happy to answer any questions you have.

[The prepared statement of Mr. Flack follows:]

Statement of Gary Flack, Chairman, Social Security Section, Federal Bar Association, Atlanta, Georgia Chairman McCrery, Representative Levin and Members of the Subcommittee:

The Social Security Section of the Federal Bar Association (FBA) welcomes this opportunity to share our thoughts about the new final regulations changing the disability claims process, the "Disability Service Improvement" (DSI) initiative. This testimony is submitted on behalf of the Social Security Section of the FBA. I am the chair of the Social Security Section of the Federal Bar Association, and this testimony does not necessarily represent the views of the national organization.

As you know, the FBA is the foremost national association of private and government lawyers engaged in practice before the federal courts and federal agencies. Sixteen thousand members of the legal profession belong to the FBA. There are also within the FBA over a dozen sections organized by substantive areas of practice, including the Social Security Section. The FBA's Social Security Section is unlike other organizations of lawyers associated with a particular constituency of Social Security disability lawyers. Our members include attorneys involved in all aspects of Social Security disability adjudication, including attorney representatives of claimants, administrative law judges, Appeals Council judges, staff attorneys in the SSA Office of Hearings and Appeals and Office of General Counsel, U.S. Attorneys and U.S. Magistrate Judges, District Court Judges and Circuit Court Judges.

Social Security Administration Commissioner Jo Anne B. Barnhart issued a final rule establishing a new disability determination process on March 31, 2006. 71 Fed. Reg. 16424 (Mar. 31, 2006). This rule is the culmination of much analysis, thought, and hard work. The Commissioner is to be congratulated for recognizing that the administrative process she inherited failed to efficiently and accurately identify many disabled claimants. She conferred with representatives of many groups, including our Section, that are interested and involved in the agency's disability determination process. The final rule reflects the input from almost 900 individuals and groups; their comments were made in response to the Commissioner's proposed rule.

This Subcommittee is also to be congratulated for its oversight role in conducting hearings on the problem and now the solution. Today, we focus our testimony on four aspects of the final rule:

- Will the reviewing official delay proceedings or become an institutional hurdle claimants must overcome?
- How should the success of DSI be measured?
- Will Region I predict how well DSI will function elsewhere?
- Will the Decision Review Board undermine the independence of ALJs?

WILL THE REVIEWING OFFICIAL DELAY PROCEEDING OR BECOME AN INSTITUTIONAL HURDLE CLAIMANTS MUST OVERCOME?

The Reviewing Official (RO) replaces the Reconsideration level of review. It appears to be a more informal, but federally-controlled decision maker. The FBA is concerned that the RO will be quickly overburdened and delay the process of developing accurate decisions. The RO is likely to need updated information, outside consultative examinations, and (if the RO contemplates paying benefits) the opinion of the new medical and vocational expert system. Unless there are as many ROs as there are Administrative Law Judges (ALJs), the caseload of each RO will soon equal or exceed the average ALJ caseload. Too large a caseload will not only delay decisionmaking, but also interfere with accurate decisionmaking. The RO may become a bottleneck, particularly since the RO must write his own detailed decision. Accordingly, we believe there should be more ROs than ALJs to move cases expeditiously.

There also may be undue delays associated with consultative examinations and permitting claimants to share these consults with their treating physicians. This process may work well with represented claimants. However, it is unclear how *pro se* claimants who are illiterate or computer-illiterate will handle electronic files or view the new consults. DSI does not specifically address these claimants in its new rules.

In addition, there may be a tendency for the RO decision to become an institutional standard in disability determinations. Some ALJs may utilize it to deny benefits. Other ALJs may regard it as a hurdle to overcome. If an ALJ reverses the RO's decision, the Decision Review Board (DRB) may question that decision based on the RO decision. The DSI must provide procedural guarantees to assure the independence of ALJs decisionmaking. It is the fair hearing that is the centerpiece of the disability adjudication process, not the RO.

Finally, we understand that initially all the ROs will be located in Falls Church, Virginia. This might make sense with the participation of one small region as a pilot project. However, as the DSI expands and the RO workforce grows to a size of at least 1100 ROs, we believe RO dispersal throughout the country should be considered. They could still review claims nationwide. There is likely to be a better pool of qualified applicants available if the Commissioner were to place them at regional locations. There are also less expensive places to live than Falls Church. In short, whatever the advantages of initially housing ROs in one location, we believe that decentralization of the RO workforce around the country should be pursued after the completion of the pilot project phase.

HOW SHOULD THE SUCCESS OF DSI BE MEASURED?

There are two primary measures of the success of DSI, involving the payment of claims by the Reviewing Official and the dynamics of judicial review.

Payment of Claims by the Reviewing Official

The purpose of the RO is to make the correct decision sooner. Accordingly, more claimants cases should be approved at the initial and RO levels than are currently approved through the reconsideration level. Fewer cases should appear for adjudication at the ALJ level. DSI can be regarded as a success if relatively more claims are paid initially at the RO level.

Dynamics of Judicial Review

After the DRB approves an ALJ decision, there are several other measures of the success of DSI.

- Do voluntary remands of federal complaints decrease after the abolition of the Appeals Council?
- Are there fewer technical errors? (For example, lost files, blank CDs etc.)
- Are there fewer obvious substantive mistakes than before? (For example, failures to follow the treating physician rule, improper uses of vocational experts, etc.)

- Is there a reduced percentage of substantive court decisions in favor of plaintiffs?
- Are there fewer "sentence 6" remands because "new and material evidence" is appropriately added to the record via the discretion of the ALJ?

Even with a faster administrative processing time, it is likely to take at least a year for cases to work their way to a final administrative denial. It will probably take another year for the first cases to proceed through federal District Court review. Thus, it is likely to take an additional two years to get one full year's worth of substantive decisions from the district courts of Region I. If the DSI process starts in August 2006, it will be approximately August 2009 before we have a year's worth of substantive judicial decisions. We wonder whether the Commissioner will delay extending the new regulations to other regions for three years, i.e. until there is one year's worth of substantive decisions from Region I.

WILL REGION I PREDICT HOW WELL DSI WILL WORK ELSEWHERE

Region I of the Social Security Administration is comprised of the States of Maine, New Hampshire, Vermont, Massachusetts, Rhode Island and Connecticut. We are concerned that Region I may not be typical of how Social Security disability claims are processed in the rest of the country. We believe, based on anecdotal and empirical evidence, that: more Region I claims are favorably decided at the initial and reconsideration levels; the ALJs are efficient and more likely to make accurate decisions; relatively few cases are appealed to federal court. Thus, we conclude that the pilot project may work well in Region I, but poorly elsewhere.

Region I is one of the smaller regions in the country in the number of ALJs (approximately 50) and in the number of new cases ALJs receive. In a recent quarter, Region I ALJs disposed of almost 1300 more cases than it received. Only Region III, a much larger Region, disposed of a greater number of cases than it received. Region III handles many more cases, absolutely, and presumably with more ALJs. Most of the other Regions disposed of fewer cases than each received, i.e., the ALJ caseload of most Regions increased.

Region I handles approximately 3% of the total number of new applications filed throughout the country. While we applaud the concept of DSI, very few claimants will obtain any benefit from the new rules so long as they are applied only in Region I, despite the increasing numbers of claimants in the system with claims awaiting evaluation.

We have attached the state-by-state allowance rate for initial and reconsidered claims (See Appendix 1). New Hampshire has initial allowance rates in excess of 60%. Massachusetts and Rhode Island initially allows about 46% of initial claims and 54% of reconsidered claims; Vermont allows about 45% of initial claims. Maine and Connecticut are somewhat lower at 38% and 19% respectively for initial and reconsidered claims. However, the favorable initial and reconsidered decision rates for Connecticut and Maine (the lowest of the Region I States) appear to be higher than national average.

Region I is a small, efficient region that approves a higher than average percentage of claims both initially and at the reconsideration level. ALJs in Maine ruled in favor of claimants in 77% of their decisions in the year ending September 26, 2003. Rhode Island had the lowest ALJ allowance rate in Region I. Its ALJs ruled in favor of 60% of the claimants. Region I has one of the highest ALJ allowance rates in the nation. (See Appendix 2)

Perhaps for these reasons, relatively few cases in Region I historically have gone to federal court: only 322 in the entire Region I. (See Appendix 3, statistics from the Administrative Office of the U.S. Courts regarding Social Security law from the Region I States in the most recent 12-month period, ending March 2005). The District Court outcomes in Region I may not be statistically significant because of the small caseload. It is not self-evident that this is the most typical region to try out the DSI reforms.

We have no information about whether Region I adjudicates an "average" range of cases including sickle cell, mental impairments, mental retardation, illiteracy? SSA will need to track this.

WILL THE DECISION REVIEW BOARD UNDERMINE THE INDEPENDENCE OF ALJ'S

The Commissioner intends the DSI to provide quality assurance throughout the Social Security disability adjudication process. The DSI is to be neutral in that the same number of applicants will be entitled to benefits at the end of the new DSI reforms as under the current system. The means to assure that the number of new claims granted remains the same must be the quality controls and the Disability Review Board (DRB).

The precise mechanism for quality assurance of the DRB is the "computer-based predictive model." We understand the Commissioner will soon sign a contract to hire outside help to devise this model. After initially evaluating 100% of all ALJ decisions, the computer-based predictive model will tell the DRB which cases to more closely evaluate. Even at the beginning, we understand that not all cases will be evaluated equally closely.

We fear that the DRB will intrude on the traditional independence of ALJs and undermine the benefits of a fair hearing. ALJs worry that the benefits of a fair hearing will be overturned by a review board that did not see the claimant or attend the hearing. Private practitioners worry that the computer program, not the individual ALJ, will become the *de facto* decision maker. The computer-based predictive model probably will not be as blunt as the discredited Bellmon review[1], but will shape ALJ decisions.

The computer-based predictive model must be a screening tool. It must be merit-based, not budget-based. It cannot be utilized to deny claims so that DSI is budget neutral. DSI may result in some increase in costs. (If claimants are paid earlier, some of the denied would die or not appeal their denial even though actually disabled. This especially applies to those with mental impairments.)

The computer-based predictive model must also be transparent. ALJs and attorneys of claimants alike are entitled to know which cases will be more closely reviewed. Presumably the case of an elderly person with lung cancer, whom an ALJ finds disabled, need not be reviewed as thoroughly as a younger individual with a bad back. However, the independent decision of the ALJ as to each must stand. Quality assurance is an admirable goal, but not at the cost of ALJ independence.

Some of our members are concerned that the predictions of a computer model will replace the judicious weighing of evidence. Others worry that this computer review will be utilized to discipline ALJs whose decisions are too different from the norm. The computer-based predictive model must not be utilized to assure that the same number of people will be entitled to benefits at the end of the new DSI reforms as under the current system. This would be a gross misuse of a quality assurance program.

Finally, at the Subcommittee's hearing on the SSA's proposed regulations last September, the Honorable Judge Howard D. McKibben, chairman of the Judicial Conference Committee on Federal-State Jurisdiction, testified about the potential increase in the number of complaints filed in federal court due to the abolishment of the Appeals Council. It is not assured that the DRB will eliminate unfortunate ALJ errors. The Commissioner has not really addressed Judge McKibben's comments.

CONCLUSION

Thank you once again for the opportunity to appear before you today. The Social Security Section of the Federal Bar Association looks forward to continuing to work with you and the Social Security Administration in improving the disability hearing process. I would be happy to answer any questions you may have.

Chairman MCCRERY. Thank you all for your testimony.

You've all brought to light some concerns that you have about the proposal by the Commissioner.

Mr. Robertson, I think the process of analyzing and examining how this rollout is working, first in the Boston Region and then later in other regions, takes on even more importance than it otherwise might because of the dramatic changes in the process that are proposed, and in the concerns that have been raised by folks who are intimately involved in the current process.

---

[1] "[T]he agency [SSA] instituted the 'Bellmon review,' a surveillance program of judges thought to be granting too many disability claims. The effect of the Bellmon review on judicial independence was chilling." Christine M. Moore, *SSA Disability Adjudication in Crisis!* 33 Judges' J. (No. 3) 2, 9 (1994). It should be emphasized that this Social Security Administration process of "own-motion review" of ALJ decisions resulted from stated Congressional concern [expressed in the 1980 Social Security Disability Amendments, Pub. L. No. 96–265, known as the "Bellmon Amendment" after Senator Henry Bellmon (D–Okla.). *See Association of Admin. Law Judges v. Heckler*, 594 F. Supp. 1132 (D.D.C. 1984) for an explanation of the legislation] at the high rate of ALJ reversal of state-level denials of claims and the variance of rates among ALJs. http://review.law.mercer.edu/old/46201ft.htm

With that in mind, what is your assessment, from the GAO's standpoint, of the Commissioner's dynamic management model that she mentioned when I asked her about the protocol for reviewing and analyzing the progress in Region I, in the Boston Region?

She said, we're going to use dynamic management, which basically I understood her to say is kind of analyzing as we go, and tweaking as we go.

What is your assessment of the efficacy of that model?

Mr. ROBERTSON. A couple quick comments on that.

Number one, we don't really have a lot of the details of just how the SSA is going to go about doing its evaluation.

You know, they have a notion of, okay, we need to do this, this, and this, but they're pretty vague on the measures they use and the timeline, that type of thing.

So, that's one point.

The other point would be just to say, "Well, here's what I think should be happening in terms of an evaluation," and I think—and perhaps I'm oversimplifying things, but sometimes that's a good thing—I think they've got to do at least three things.

They've got to look at the individual components of the new system and determine whether or not they're working the way they were supposed to work.

In other words, are the Quick Disability Determination (QDD) actually producing decisions quickly at the front end? If you're looking at the back end, again, you'd be looking at, well, what's happening and how effectively is the DRB doing its thing?

So, that would be one kind of a micro look at the individual components of the new system. That's got to be done, and that's got to be done continuously so they can tweak the system as the rollout occurs.

The more macro level evaluation, and this is so very, very important, is to remember there was a purpose, there were broad objectives for this system right from the get-go, and they were to improve the timeliness of the decisionmaking process and improve the consistency and make sure the decisions were fair.

Somehow, at some point in time, SSA needs to flesh out just exactly how they're going to do that, and I say that now because if they don't do that, a year or two from now you hold hearings and you ask me or you ask the commissioner, "Well, how are things going with the new rollout?"

You know, we wouldn't, if we didn't have a good evaluation system in place, we wouldn't be able to say, or we'd be saying, "Well, some things look good but we really didn't have the right measures, or we didn't measure the right things," that type of thing.

So, the second part of it is making sure that we're accomplishing the overall objectives or evaluating the overall objectives of the DSI.

Last but certainly not least is, we need to have an idea of how much all this costs.

So, basically, it boils down really to two things: is the DSI working as intended, both on the macro and micro level; and how much is it costing us?

Chairman MCCRERY. It seems to me that the first two things should be fairly easy to measure, particularly in comparison to where we are now and the system that exists now.

The third component of your micro list, though, are the decisions fair, I don't know who is going to decide that. I don't know that you can——

Mr. ROBERTSON. I don't know how that's going to transpire.

Chairman MCCRERY. —measure that, but the first two I think are imminently measurable and can be done.

The question of cost, almost everybody here has raised the issue of are there sufficient resources available to allow this reform to work. Have you made any assessment of that, given the resources that are available?

Mr. ROBERTSON. At this point in our review,we haven't looked at the costs. You know, we have the figures that SSA had in the final rule, but that's the extent of it.

Chairman MCCRERY. Okay. Before I turn it over to Mr. Levin, I thought each of you were very clear in your testimony. I don't have a lot of questions. A lot of these questions that the staff prepared were answered, I thought, pretty well.

I want us to keep in mind, though, that the reason we're all here and the reason the Commissioner has been doing this is because the current system really hasn't worked very well, and the current system is not very fair, just in terms of the process to claimants, because they have to wait so dadgum long to get a decision, any decision.

That's what we're all trying to get at, and the Commissioner has done her best at coming up with a new process that she hopes will give claimants a better shake.

We don't know if it's going to work, and that's why we want to hear from you all, so that we can get as much input going in to anticipate problems.

Then we also want to get in place a rigorous assessment protocol so we can tell as we're going along whether things are working.

Then last, we want to try to make sure—this is probably the most difficult part—that sufficient resources are made available to allow the process that she's come up with to work as she's designed it, and that, unfortunately, to some extent, we have to leave up to the appropriators.

Mr. Levin and I both have been very adamant in our requests to the appropriators for more funding, and unfortunately, they didn't give us what we asked for, but we'll continue to beat on them and see if we can help get some more resources.

I appreciate very much the input that you all have provided not only today but prior to today as the Commissioner is developing a process and making changes to it.

So, thank you very much.

Mr. Levin.

Mr. LEVIN. Maybe I'll pick up on that statement, because the staff, with its usual efficiency, has outlined all kinds of questions, and maybe what we should do is to present them to you in writing so that each of you can give us your inputs, how the system works at every step.

I guess I just want to say that in the end, the test is not only the quality, but how we address the backlog.

In Mr. Hill's testimony, and the commissioner went as far as I think she could under the constraints, 727,000 cases pending? Isn't one of the tests of any system going to be its reduction? I would think so.

The average processing time of 480 days—I'm not quite sure what that all means, from beginning to end. That's a lot of cases that have a long time to be processed now.

I think that's outrageous.

The Chairman has very much joined in, and I think has really led the way to try to bring attention to this.

So, we'll ask you a lot of detailed questions, and if you'll answer them, but I do think we need to signal that the test of the new system will be whether it addresses this and if not, why not; and I do think that part of the answer is going to be resources.

I don't see how any system, no matter how well designed, works without resources.

Maybe we use this analogy too often, because I come from Michigan, but, it doesn't really matter how well a car runs if there's no gasoline, whatever the resource, whatever the source of the gasoline—I should use "of the fuel," I shouldn't say gasoline, fuel.

So, I think we should put ourselves on notice that if there isn't a substantial reduction of this, and so I'll just ask any of you point-blank, are any of you confident that this new system will mean in a couple of years a dramatic reduction in the number of pending cases?

I guess since it's starting in one region, the answer is there can't be right in a short period of time, right?

How about 3 years from now? What's the plan? How quickly is this supposed to be spread to other places? Do we know that?

Mr. SKWIERCZYNSKI. Well, I don't think the commissioner has laid out exactly the rollout strategy.

We in the American Federal government Employees (AFGE) union think that she put the cart before the horse. There are different options that one could use to improve the disability process. She's decided on an option, issued regulations, and now it's done, and they haven't even tested it.

That's a dangerous step to take, to without any testing or piloting, to issue regulations and say, "Here's the process."

Now, during the redesign experiment, people, the consumers of this disability program, disabled people said they want a caseworker approach. Why isn't this being piloted? Why didn't the commissioner look at a caseworker approach, where the person you deal with makes the decision? Makes it more user friendly, not adds but removes some of the litigation.

When you have a litigious process, it's going to take time, it's going to take a lot more time writing a lengthy decision that another appellate—at another appellate level has to be rebutted, and then both of those decisions go to another appellate level and you create a conflict. That's going to take a lot of time, right through that process.

So, I don't see this at all cutting down backlogs.

One thing that was done, you certainly, if you strip the last appellate level, you're going to shorten the end point. You know, you're going to get to court quicker, because you've sliced an appeal.

As I testified, that particular appeal, the Appeals Council had a 30 percent remand and reversal rate, so there's a lot of people who their cases will probably be decided in error because they couldn't avail themselves of that appeal.

I don't know that that's where we want to go, to shorten the process and ensure that a certain segment of the claims are going to be decided erroneously. I don't see where that gets to where we want to go.

Mr. HILL. The implementation schedule is lengthy. I think today the commissioner mentioned something about 5 years.

Mr. LEVIN. Right.

Mr. HILL. I think that the schedule, as I——

Mr. LEVIN. With adequate resources, she said.

Mr. HILL. As I understand it, there will be—Region I starts, it will be a year. If everything goes well, then it will be rolled out in Region 8, then Region 10, then Region 7. Those are our four smallest regions. I don't know the timeframe for the rest.

I think when you have rolled out those four regions, you will probably have less than 20 percent of the hearing office workload in DSI hearing offices. The other 80 percent will still be under the old system.

So, I suspect there's quite a lengthy period of time before we are going to—we in Region 5—I'm from Ohio—I don't think we'll see it for 4 years. We are the second biggest region. We're probably going to be near the last.

Ms. FORD. I'd like to comment. From the perspective of claimants, the Commissioner has gone after some very critical issues here in terms of developing better evidence earlier in the process, and moving some of the cases more quickly through the system.

I think the new FedRO level is designed to help get at the evidence issue. The FedRO will have subpoena power. Now, claimants and their representatives don't have any control over whether they can get that evidence and how quickly they can get it.

So, I think she is going after some of the key pieces, and in good faith, is looking at trying to improve the system up front.

I think it's absolutely critical that—and I hope my testimony made this clear—it's absolutely critical that all the players be involved from this point on in terms of observing what is happening, provide feedback to the SSA and to the Subcommittee, and maintain that continual loop of information so that where there are problems they can be addressed quickly.

I wouldn't want to see a problem go down the road very far and have a lot of people affected by it if there were a way that we could catch it early.

So, I see it as a dynamic process that we all participate in, and that we have a responsibility to participate in.

Thank you.

Mr. LEVIN. Yes, sir? Is it all right if we keep going?

Chairman MCCRERY. Sure.

Mr. LEVIN. Yes, sir.

Mr. BERNOSKI. Yes. I was just going to add that the—I think the backlogs will be here, these large number of cases, for some time in the future, but also, these backlogs to a large extent are created by other factors that are outside the control of the SSA, such as the economic condition.

We know when the economic conditions have a downturn, it seems that we have more filings, so we have more cases that we have to handle—the demographics of the population.

So, there are these other factors that affect the number of cases that come into the system, and it's not that the people aren't working hard like the commissioner indicated.

The ALJ and the assistant and the people, and not only the judges, but the other people in the Office of Hearings and Appeals, last year, we disposed of about 600,000 cases.

That's a lot of cases when you consider you're taking these one at a time. That's kind of the albatross in this system. We have 725,000 cases. We hear them one at a time. We don't package them. That's a big job.

There's other factors that impinge upon it that no one really has any control over.

Mr. LEVIN. Well, when you say no control, I think it would mean if there are more cases, you need more resources to handle the cases, so it isn't quite that we have no control over it. It means we're not controlling.

Mr. BERNOSKI. Precisely. We don't have any control over the cases that are coming into the system.

Mr. LEVIN. So, whatever the differences might be about this experiment, it would seem essential that there be adequate resources for both an introduction of a new system and for the utility, the implementation of the old system. and as you say, Ms. Ford, adequate participation by everybody in implementing a new system.

So, I think we better leave here today, I think all of you believe that there has to be adequate resources to make a system work. This is not an acceptable backlog, is it? Should we ask you to study this?

Mr. ROBERTSON. We'd be happy to.

Mr. LEVIN. Okay. Well, we'll chat about this afterward.

Thank you very, very much, and thank you for this time. I think it's been a very useful hearing, and we leave, I think, with the sobering sense that we've got a responsibility to make sure that this agency has the resources that it needs.

Thank you, Mr. Chairman.

Chairman MCCRERY. Thank you, Mr. Levin.

Thank all of you very much once again for appearing today and sharing with us your testimony.

I'm sure we will be calling on some of you in the future as we go through this process of getting the new system in place, and we'll urge you to share with us at that time your impression of how it's going. Thank you very much.

This hearing is adjourned.

[Whereupon, at 1:00 p.m., the Subcommittee was adjourned.]

[Submissions for the record follow]

Statement of Linda Fullerton, Social Security Disability Coalition, Rochester, New York

Members of the Committee:

My name is Linda Fullerton, I am permanently disabled and receive Social Security Disability Insurance/SSDI and Medicare. I am also President/Co-Founder of the Social Security Disability Coalition, which is made up of thousands of Social Security Disability claimants and recipients from all over the nation. Our group and experiences, are a very accurate reflection and microcosm of what is happening to millions of Social Security Disability applicants all over this nation. I must take this opportunity to tell you how very proud I am of all our members, many like myself, whose own lives have been devastated by a system that was set up to help them. In spite of that, they are using what very little time and energy they can muster due to their own disabilities, to try and help other disabled Americans survive the nightmare of applying for Social Security Disability benefits. There is no better example of the American spirit than these extraordinary people! If you visit the Social Security Disability Coalition website, or the Social Security Disability Reform petition website:

Social Security Disability Coalition-offering FREE knowledge and support with a focus on SSD reform:

http://group.msn.com/SocialSecurityDisabilityColition

Sign the Social Security Disability Reform Petition-read the horror stories from all over the nation:

http://www.petitiononline.com/SSDC/petition.html

You will read over three years worth of documented horror stories and see thousands of signatures of disabled Americans whose lives have been harmed by the Social Security Disability program. You cannot leave without seeing the excruciating pain and suffering that these people have been put through just because they happened to become disabled, and went to their government to file a claim for disability insurance that they worked so very hard to pay for. I continually throughout the Commissioner's Disability New Approach Program sent her hundreds of their stories/comments from our website and petition and yet nowhere in her DSI plan do I see any real help/relief for them.

My organization fills a void that is greatly lacking in the SSA claims process. While we never represent claimants in their individual cases, and in most cases due the nature of our group, we don't even know their real names for privacy concerns, we are still able to provide claimants with much needed support and resources to guide them through the nebulous maze that is put in front of them when applying for SSDI/SSI benefits. In spite of the fact that the current system is not conducive to case worker, client interaction other than the initial claims intake, we continue to encourage claimants to communicate as much as possible with the SSA in order to speed up the claims process, making it easier on both the SSA caseworkers and the claimants themselves. As a result we are seeing claimants getting their cases approved on their own without the need for paid attorneys, and when additional assistance is needed we connect them with FREE resources to represent them should their cases advance to the hearing phase. We also provide them with information on how to access available assistance to help them cope with every aspect of their lives that may be affected by the enormous wait time that it currently takes to process an SSDI/SSI claim, including where to get Medicaid and other State/Federal programs, also free/low cost healthcare, medicine, food, housing, financial assistance and too many other things to mention here. We educate them in the policies and regulations which govern the SSDI/SSI process and connect them to the answers for the many questions they have about how to access their disability benefits in a timely manner, relying heavily on the SSA website to provide this help. If we as disabled Americans, who are not able to work because we are so sick ourselves, can come together, using absolutely no money and with very little time or effort can accomplish these things, how is it that the SSA which is funded by our taxpayer dollars fails so miserably at this task?

The Social Security Disability New Approach Program at its inception, was a welcome change from what we have seen in decades past. Everyone that I have dealt with on the Commissioner's staff was very courteous and responsive to our concerns at the time and I am very grateful for that. We kept in constant communication with them as much as we were allowed to participate. I have also been privileged to interact with other employees of the SSA who have been of great help to my organization as well, in particular members of AFGE/National Council Of SSA Field Operations Locals American Federation Of Government Employees. In spite of my own personal nightmare SSDI claims experience which I will be describing, and the horror stories I hear on a daily basis, I am well aware that there are very hard working, committed, caring people who work for this program. One of our goals is to increase the lines of communication between the SSA and the disabled community.

That being said, DSI does not go far enough, fast enough for those who desperately need to access disability benefits and whose very lives depend on them. It greatly disappoints me that the Commissioner has not addressed most of the problems that my organization, and hundreds of others had alerted her office about as part of the SS Disability New Approach Program, in fact our cries for help have been virtually ignored when making her recent regulation changes. I find it to be a shame and disservice to the American taxpayers. It seems that the regulations that have now been put in place will not do very much if anything to relieve this horrendous situation, and for the most part will be very detrimental to the disability claims process, rather than improve it. As mentioned, I have been in direct communications with AFGE/National Council Of SSA Field Operations Locals American Federation Of Government Employees, AFL–CIO who represents thousands of Social Security Workers for the past few years now and we have been trying together to clean up the problems that would make the disability claims process better for both sides—the disability claimants and the SSA workers themselves. It is amazing, and very refreshing to learn about how much we agree, on the changes needed to make the SSDI/SSI process easier. They have been extremely helpful to my group which has allowed me to better help those struggling to get these crucial benefits. If we can do these things together I see no reason why the SSA Commissioner (if she was doing her job properly) would not want us actively involved every step of the way in these changes that she is making. While I know the SSA is doing their very best with the resources they have, they cannot do it alone, as many things needed to truly reform this system, must be legislated by Congress. So I call on you today to start taking this crisis seriously as many lives literally depend on your actions.

As a person who has gone through the Social Security Disability claims process myself, I know first hand about the pain, financial, physical and emotional devastation that the current problematic SSDI process can cause, and I will never be able to recover from it, since I can no longer work. I find it disturbing that at this latest hearing and at past hearings, that glaringly absent from your panel was representation from other disability organizations such as mine. You continually choose the same panelists from the disability community when there is any representation at all. I ask again as I have in the past, that in future Congressional hearings on these matters, that I be allowed to actively participate instead of being forced to always submit testimony in writing, after the main hearing takes place. I am more than willing to testify in person before Congress and I should be permitted to do so. I want a major role in the Social Security Disability reformation process, since any changes that occur have a direct major impact on my life and our members lives and well being. Who better to give feedback at these hearings than those who are directly affected by its flaws! A more concerted effort needs to be utilized when scheduling future hearings, factoring in enough time to allow panelists that better represent a wider cross section of the American population, to testify in person. It seems to me that if this is not done, that you are not getting a total reflection of the population affected, and are making decisions on inaccurate information which can be very detrimental to those whom you have been elected to serve.

From GAO testimony to your committee on 6/15/06: "Finally, SSA's communication efforts with stakeholders align with change management principles in several respects. For example, SSA has employed a proactive, collaborative approach to engaging the stakeholder community both during DSI's design and in its planning for implementation in order to explain why change is necessary, workable, and beneficial. Even before the notice of proposed rule making on DSI was published, SSA began to meet with stakeholder groups to develop the proposal that would eventually shape the new structure. Then, once the proposed rule was issued, SSA officials told us they formed a team to read and analyze the hundreds of comment letters that stakeholders submitted. In addition, they conducted a number of meetings with external stakeholders to help the agency identify common areas of concern and develop an approach to resolving the issues stakeholders raised before rollout began. According to SSA officials responsible for these meetings, the Commissioner attended more than 100 meetings to hear stakeholder concerns directly. Further, SSA recently scheduled a meeting for early July with claimant representatives to discuss that group's particular concerns about how the new process will affect their work and their disability clients. SSA officials told us that senior-level staff will lead the meeting and that about 100 claimant representatives from the Boston region will attend."

"While SSA's steps and plans look promising, we want to stress the importance of diligence and follow-through in two key areas. The first is quality assurance, which entails both effective monitoring and evaluation. A solid monitoring plan is key to helping SSA quickly identify and correct problems that surface in the Boston rollout, because any failure to correct problems could put the entire process at risk. An evaluation plan is critical for ensuring that processes are working as intended and that SSA is achieving its overarching goals of making accurate, consistent decisions as early in the process as possible. The second key area is communication. It is important for SSA's top leadership to support open lines of communication throughout implementation if the agency is to facilitate a successful transition. Failure to, for example, provide useful feedback to staff—many of whom will be new to the agency or at least to the new tools—could significantly jeopardize opportunities for improvement. Just as important, SSA's top management needs to ensure that the concerns and questions of stakeholders affected by the new process are heard, and that concerned parties are kept apprised of how SSA intends to respond."

It does not seem to me that SSA is off to a very good start in that area. I continually asked to be part of such meetings if and when they were ever held, but was never informed of any them, thus was not allowed to participate. Since my organization primarily consists of SSDI/SSI claimants, I have to question what sorts of "stakeholders" the Commissioner met with. Seems like her main concern is to meet with "stakeholders" who stand to make the most money from a claimant's problems with the SSDI/SSI program rather than the claimant's themselves who are most affected by those problems. This is further evidenced by the list of "stakeholders" referenced in the aforementioned GAO testimony. Again proof of the Federal Government catering to special interest groups. While many of these "claimant representatives" may have good intentions, unless they personally experience what it is actually like to live through the process of applying for these benefits, and have their lives permanently altered as a result of it, they can never accurately convey to anyone what the problems with dealing with a severely broken system is like for us. If this system is ever to be reformed properly, it is crucial that before any changes to this program are implemented, that the majority of input/involvement in any phase of change be with a team of actual SSDI/SSI claimants and the SSA workers themselves who must implement any proposed changes.

The Commissioner in the past has stated "In drafting this final rule, we understood that, although there was broad agreement on the need for change, numerous commenters perceived our proposed rule as favoring administrative efficiency over fairness."

It is very detrimental to the American people, if the Commissioner is using their hard earned money to harm them for the sake of efficiency rather than make it a priority to take every step necessary to see that their cases are processed fairly as well as quickly. We fear rubberstamping of denials for the sake of efficiency, which is in fact ignoring the will of the people.

It is my understanding that Congressman Levin suggested during the hearing that the General Accounting Office (GAO) should conduct a study and cost analysis of DSI. After my own personal experience with filing a claim for SSDI benefits dealing with enormous processing time and the totally unnecessary problems I encountered, I also agree that their should be major oversight by an independent body of all phases of the disability claims process. I agree with the Congressman that the GAO would do well to be involved in investigating further how the Commissioner's proposals would not only affect the SSA, but more importantly how her proposals would affect the claimant's themselves, which after all our input, she continues to ignore.

We ask that the GAO review processing times of all phases of the disability claims process with particular focus on the DDS offices and the ALJ's where the largest bottlenecks and inconsistencies in the program are found. In addition we want the GAO to consider recommending to Congress that they move to legislate that the Federal Government take over the role that the DDS offices now perform. We have seen a wide range of denial/approval rates and processing times for the same classifications of disabilities based entirely on the state in which a claimant lives, or which DDS worker (their training is very inconsistent by state) happens to handle their claim. This should not be allowed and in fact most people including elected officials are not aware that DDS workers are state, rather than Federal employees. It is widely known that the following Federal Standards are not being met by the DDS offices as the program is currently structured:

404.1642 Processing time standards http://www.ssa.gov/OP_Home/cfr20/404/404-1642.htm

(a) General. Title II processing time refers to the average number of days, including Saturdays, Sundays, and holidays, it takes a State agency to process an initial disability claim from the day the case folder is received in the State agency until the day it is released to us by the State agency. Title XVI processing time refers to the average number of days, including Saturdays, Sundays, and holidays, from the day of receipt of the initial disability claim in the State agency until systems input of a presumptive disability decision or the day the case folder is released to us by the State agency, whichever is earlier.

(b) Target levels. The processing time target levels are:

(1) 37 days for title II initial claims.

(2) 43 days for title XVI initial claims.

(c) Threshold levels. The processing time threshold levels are:

(1) 49.5 days for title II initial claims.

(2) 57.9 days for title XVI initial claims. [46 FR 29204, May 29, 1981, as amended at 56 FR 11020, Mar. 14, 1991]

404.1643 Performance accuracy standard http://www.ssa.gov/OP_Home/cfr20/404/404–1643.htm

(a) General. Performance accuracy refers to the percentage of cases that do not have to be returned to State agencies for further development or correction of decisions based on evidence in the files and as such represents the reliability of State agency adjudication. The definition of performance accuracy includes the measurement of factors that have a potential for affecting a decision, as well as the correctness of the decision. For example, if a particular item of medical evidence should have been in the file but was not included, even though its inclusion does not change the result in the case, that is a performance error. Performance accuracy, therefore, is a higher standard than decisional accuracy. As a result, the percentage of correct decisions is significantly higher than what is reflected in the error rate established by SSA's quality assurance system.

(b) Target level. The State agency initial performance accuracy target level for combined title II and title XVI cases is 97 percent with a corresponding decision accuracy rate of 99 percent.

(c) Intermediate Goals. These goals will be established annually by SSA's regional commissioner after negotiation with the State and should be used as stepping stones to progress towards our targeted level of performance.

(d) Threshold levels. The State agency initial performance accuracy threshold level for combined title II and title XVI cases is 90.6 percent.

The following GAO reports over the past several years prove that there are major problems with this program:

GAO–04–656—More Effort Needed To Assess Consistency of Disability Decisions—July 2004

GAO–03–117—Social Security Administration: Major Management Challenges and Program Risks—January 2003

GAO–03–119—High Risk Series: An Update—January 2003

GAO–02–826T—Social Security Disability: Significant Problems Persist and Difficult Decisions Lie Ahead

GAO–02–322—Disappointing Results From SSA's Efforts to Improve the Disability Claims Process Warrant Immediate Attention

GAO/HEHS–97–28—APPEALED DISABILITY CLAIMS: Despite SSA's Efforts It Will Not Reach Backlog Reduction Goal

GAO/HRD–94–11—Increasing Number of Disability Claims and Deteriorating Service

GAO/HEHS–94–34—Disability Rolls Keep Growing While Explanations Remain Elusive

Productivity/Poor Customer Service

The Commissioner has stated: "SSA is a good and worthy investment. Our achievements over the last year are proof that resources provided to SSA are used efficiently and effectively to administer America's social security programs."

It is very true that SSA is a good and worthy investment when it works properly to provide vital disability benefits to claimants in a timely manner, but from the Federal regulations that are violated on a daily basis and the GAO reports to date, this is not the case at all. This statement shows that the Commissioner is totally out of touch with what is happening on her watch. I would be more that willing to speculate that any other corporation in this country who ran their business this poorly, would be out of business in it's first year! By client standards SSA customer service is extremely poor and in major need of improvement across the board. Here is just a small sampling of the constant complaints we receive about the Social Security Disability system and its employees:

Severe understaffing of SSD workers at all levels of the program

Extraordinary wait times between the different phases of the disability claims process

Employees being rude/insensitive to claimants

Employees outright refusing to provide information to claimants or do not have the knowledge to do so

Employees not returning calls

Employees greatly lacking in knowledge of and in some cases purposely violating Social Security and Federal Regulations (including Freedom of Information Act and SSD Pre-Hearing review process).

Claimants getting conflicting/erroneous information depending on whom they happen to talk to at Social Security—causing confusion for claimants and in some cases major problems including improper payments

Complaints of lack of attention or totally ignoring-medical records provided and claimants concerns by Field Officers, IME doctors and ALJ's

Fraud on the part of DDS/OHA offices, ALJ's IME's-purposely manipulating/ignoring information provided to deny claims

Complaints of having lost files and files being purposely thrown in the trash

Complaints of having other claimants information improperly filed/mixed in where it doesn't belong causing breach of security

Complaints of backlogs at payment processing center for initial payments once claim is approved

Federal Quality Review process adding more wait time to claims processing, increasing backlogs, no ability to follow up in this phase

Poor/little coordination if information between the different departments and phases of disability process

Note: These complaints refer to all phases of the SSD process including local office, Disability Determinations, Office of Hearing and Appeals, Payment Processing Center and the Social Security main office in MD (800 number)

All these concerns were submitted in writing by myself, to the Commissioner's staff as part of the New Approach program, and in previous testimonies to this committee, yet very few of them have even been addressed as part of the DSI. While there is no acceptable excuse for why these incidents are occurring, it is of no surprise to me that they are, based on the current conditions under which the SSA functions. I must take this time to remind you that we are not just nine digit SS numbers or case files, and I am sure as a result of very stressful working conditions, that it is very easy at times for SSA workers to forget that fact. We are living, breathing, and due to our illnesses—very fragile human beings, whose survival in most cases, totally depends on these benefits. Often we are treated like criminals on trial, or malingerers looking for a handout. Social Security Disability (SSDI) is a Federal disability INSURANCE plan—not welfare—where money is taken out of your paycheck every week, yet you could face homelessness, bankruptcy and even death trying to get your benefits when you need them most. Unfortunately, you may find yourself in a situation where you suddenly need to access this fund, then find it's the most mismanaged, problematic Federal program there is. The stories of abusive and rude behavior towards SSD/SSI claimants continue to increase. There does not seem to be much oversight in this area, which is totally unacceptable. The GAO and the SSA needs to monitor this problem more closely. A greater effort must be made to treat all claimants with the utmost respect and dignity and when necessary SSA must remove offending employees immediately. I ask that Congress/GAO create an independent oversight team to make sure these problems are corrected as soon as possible.

The SSA and GAO need to involve people such as myself who are directly affected by any changes to the SSDI/SSI program in any studies, surveys or committees to determine what changes would be in the best interest of the disability community. Nobody knows better about the flaws in the system and possible solutions to the problems, then those who are forced to go through it and deal with the consequences when it does not function properly. From my own personal experience, and those of so many others that I have come in contact with, the best approach is one that has the least amount of paperwork, the quickest processing times, the most communication with SS workers, and no need to have attorneys or the courts involved in the processing of claims. This program should be as simple as a claim for any other kind of insurance such as unemployment, auto etc. because insurance is actually what these benefits are! There is no need for it to be this burdensome, bureaucratic nightmare that it has turned into. To achieve this goal we suggest that you also establish an independent commission, again including disability program clients, to provide an ongoing monitoring/assessment of customer service, cost, time savings, and functions of the Social Security Disability program.

At this point I feel that one of the best ways to illustrate the problems with the SSDI claims process is to relate my own experience with the program. For the last 30 years of my life I contributed to the Social Security System as millions of Americans do every day. I never expected to use those funds till I was old enough to retire, yet I was personally devastated by the SSA, losing everything I worked for because I became ill. In December of 2001, I applied for Social Security Disability benefits which I assumed would be there to help me in my time of need. I'd heard nothing but discouraging stories, but figured every case was different, and anyone with the list of illnesses that I had, and the documentation to prove it, would surely get the help they needed, yet I was sorely mistaken. After filling out several pages of paperwork, which I was told was greatly reduced from which it had originally been, and submitting a huge stack of medical records supporting my claim, I was told it would take 4–6 months to go through the disability claims process. I was shocked and asked what I was supposed to live on, and I was told to apply for Social Services (Medicaid, food stamps and cash assistance) while my claim was being reviewed. I did just that, and was denied any sort of help based on the cash value of a life insurance policy that is not even enough to bury me when I die. Due to all my illnesses if I cashed in that policy, I would never be able to get that form of insurance again! Going through that process and paperwork was very difficult and humiliating as well, and then to be denied any help, just added even more to my stress and misery.

I was hoping beyond hope that I would soon get word that my disability claim was approved, but instead on 4/25/02, I got the incredible letter that my Social Security Disability claim had been denied! I found out that it's common knowledge on the streets and in legal circles that very few get approved the first time they apply. Something is extremely wrong when you have to deal with the pain and suffering physically and mentally that comes along with the illnesses you have, and then have to struggle so hard to get the benefits that you have worked for all your life.

I still couldn't understand how it was possible that anyone could read about all the medical problems I have, and it not be totally transparent that I should qualify for benefits, and that I never should've been denied in the first place! I immediately filed for an appeal, had to go through an even more complicated process and was told it would be at least August of 2003 before I got my hearing if I didn't die first! On 9/13/02, when I called the Office of Hearings and Appeals in Buffalo NY to check on my claim the receptionist told me, that my file was still in the un-worked status, which meant that nobody was assigned to my claim yet, or even looked at the file at all since March, when I originally filed my appeal. I expressed my disgust that after six months in their possession that it had not even been touched yet! I called them again on 1/23/03 and they told me that STILL nobody had been assigned to my case and it would be a MINIMUM of five months more or longer since they were just starting to work on cases that were filed in November of 2001! The receptionist expressed her sympathy for my cause and literally begged me to let others know (especially the government and media) about how much of a problem they are having. Imagine my surprise when I was calling them for help and they were begging me—a disabled person, to get them help! That just proves even further how poorly run the SSD program is. I was told that there were only 50 employees handling hundreds of thousands of cases and they, along with all of us claimants critically need help now!

Congressional offices in many cases contact Social Security on behalf their constituents going through the SSD process, so they must be aware of the many problems that exist with the program. I wrote to ALL my elected officials and as a registered voter myself, was very disappointed, disillusioned, and disgusted that my elected officials whom I have supported in the polls every year, when I asked for help in my own particular case, that the very few who responded at all, said that I needed to be become homeless or have my utilities shut off before they could help me, and there was nothing else they could do to expedite my claim. It was totally appalling and unacceptable to me, that never once, did they say that they would do anything to try and correct the flaws in the system that cause the horrors we SSDI/SSI applicants face. The bi-partisan apathy in regards to this issue is not only unacceptable, but criminally negligent behavior, and Congress needs to be held responsible for it, create the legislation and get the funding needed to address this crisis. We elected them, trusting that they would protect, serve, and be there for us in our time of need. Time is of the utmost importance in this matter, as millions of SS Disability applicants, even as I write this are suffering and losing everything, including their lives, while trying to get their benefits.

In March 2003 I called the hearings and appeals office again and they said it would be at least August 2003 before someone would look at my case. I then did some research and found out that I could request copies of the reports of the SSD IME doctor I was sent to, and the notes of the original DDS claim examiner that denied me, and when I received them, my worst allegations were then confirmed. Even though I have no real neurological problems they sent me to a neurologist to examine me, so of course he would find nothing wrong with me and say that I did not qualify as disabled. I should have instead, been sent to a Rheumatologist since most of my problems are caused by several autoimmune disorders. I also discovered that the DDS examiner purposely manipulated my medical information in order to deny my claim. Even though I filed my disability claim based on all the physical problems I have, the DDS examiner purposely wrote depression as a PRIMARY diagnosis for disability, instead of as secondary one, so of course I would be denied based on that as well. This was after I had already submitted tons of documents to prove my PHYSICAL disability—reports/documents that he chose to ignore. I then contacted the Social Security Office of Public Inquiries and the Inspector General's office in MD and filed a formal willful misconduct complaint to him against the Buffalo DDS office. In April 2003, I requested an immediate pre-hearing review of my case on the grounds of misconduct and additional physical evidence. In order to get that process going I had to fax the OHA copies of their own regulations since the person I spoke with there had no clue what I was talking about. Once they got all my paperwork to request the review, a senior staff attorney, and then a hearing and appeals judge granted my request and my case was then sent back to the DDS office that originally denied my claim. Finally it was seen by a different DDS person who actually knew how to do their job. In two weeks my case was approved at the DDS level and then was selected randomly by computer (7 out of every 10 cases get chosen) for Federal review. It then took another three weeks to be processed there.

By this time, I had wiped out my life savings and lived off my pension from a previous employer which is totally gone now, due to the enormous wait for my claim to be processed properly. One month before becoming totally bankrupt, homeless, losing my health insurance, and everything else I had worked for the last 30 years of my life, I finally won my case by myself, with no lawyer representing me, exactly 1½ years to the day from when I originally filed my claim. Under SSD regulations 5 months of my retro pay was withheld for no good reason, money I surely could have used to help pay off debts incurred while waiting for approval of my benefits. All the SSD retro pay I did received is gone now too and the benefits I do get are nowhere near enough to live on for the rest of my life. Plus there is always the stress of having to deal with the SS Continuing Disability Review Process every few years, where the threat of having your benefits suddenly cut off constantly hangs over your head, even though all my illnesses are incurable and are getting progressively worse. This is a total waste of time and money on the part of the SSA to review people with incurable, no hope for improvement conditions, such as mine.

Even after I was finally approved for benefits, since current Medicare program regulations discriminate against disabled Americans by making them wait for 24 months after their disability date of entitlement, I didn't become eligible for Medicare until June 2004, having to spend over half of my SSD check each month on health insurance premiums and prescriptions, not including the additional co-pays fees on top of it. Despite what you may hear, Social Security Disability benefits rarely cover the basis necessities of life. The American dream has become the American nightmare for me, since day to day I don't know how I'm going to survive without some miracle like winning the lottery. I'm now doomed to spend what's left of my days here on earth, living in poverty, in addition to all my medical concerns since I'm no longer able to work, and nobody in their right mind would willing choose this horrible existence.

I continually deal with enormous stress and face the continued looming threat of bankruptcy and homelessness, due to the cost of my healthcare and basic living expenses, still not qualifying for any public assistance programs. I personally hold accountable the SSA, the DDS Office in Buffalo NY, Congress and State legislators for their apathy in regards to the problems that this program has, for the mental, physical, emotional and financial destruction that this experience has cost me. I have vowed to do whatever it takes for the rest of my life, to make sure that no other American citizen has to endure the hell that I continue to live with everyday as a result of having to file for SSDI/SSI benefits. I did not ask for this fate and would trade places with a healthy person in a minute. Nobody ever thinks it can happen to them. I am proof that it can, and remember that disease and tragedy do not discriminate on the basis of age, race or sex.

America needs to wake up and take action—anyone including you, could be one step away from walking in my shoes at any moment! While the majority of Americans were shocked at the reaction of the Federal government in the aftermath of hurricane Katrina, I wasn't surprised at all. Americans saw when hurricane Katrina struck, how the poor and disabled were left to die in the streets when they needed help the most. I shudder to think of how many more lives will be further ruined or lost, when the mentally and physically disabled victims of Katrina, other natural disasters, 9/11 victims who survived that day, but are now disabled and facing a similar fate, and the other disabled Americans in general, encounter their next experience with the Federal government as they apply for their SSDI/SSI benefits. Also nothing is heard about the Veterans who are injured in the line of duty and have to go through this same scenario to get their benefits too. There are cases of Veterans rated 100% disabled by the VA who get denied their Social Security Disability benefits and end up living in poverty on the streets. Horrible treatment for those who protect and serve our country. Keep in mind a country is only as strong as the citizens that live there, yet as you can now see, the Social Security Disability process preys on the weak, and decimates the disabled population even further. The process that an applicant endures when filing for SS disability benefits, causes irreparable harm and has many serious side effects including financial and physical devastation, unbearable stress and anxiety, depression, and in some cases the depression is so severe that suicide seems to be the only option to get rid of the pain, of dealing with a system riddled with abuses against the disabled, already fragile citizens of this country. It is a known medical fact that stress of any kind can be detrimental to a person's health, and to subject a population whose health is already in jeopardy to the sorts of stress that this process can cause, further erodes a claimant's health and is Federally sanctioned torture. Based on my own personal experience, and from the horror stories I hear on a daily basis I can't help but feel that the Social Security Disability program is purposely structured to be very complicated, confusing, and with as many obstacles as possible, in order to discourage and suck the life out of claimants, hoping that they give up or die in the application process, so that benefits do not have to be paid to them. A sad commentary to say the least.

We the "Claimants, Customers, Stakeholders" are the people that the people that the SSA and Congress is supposed to be serving and listed below are some of our concerns and proposals for reform:

We want disability benefits determinations to be based solely on the physical or mental disability of the applicant. Neither age, education or any other factors should ever be considered when evaluating whether or not a person is disabled. If a person cannot work due to their medical conditions—they CAN'T work no matter what their age, or how many degrees they have, yet this is a standard practice when deciding Social Security Disability determinations. These non-disabling factors should be eliminated immediately as a factor in determining benefits eligibility.

The SSA "Bluebook" listing of diseases that qualify a person for disability should be updated more frequently to include newly discovered crippling diseases such as the many autoimmune disorders that are ravaging our citizens. Also SSD's current 3 year earnings window calculation method fails to recognize slowly progressive conditions which force people to gradually work/earn less for periods longer than 3 years, thus those with such conditions never receive their 'healthy' earnings peak rate.

In her testimony before the Senate Finance Committee on 3/14/06 the Commissioner referred to an Electronic Disability Guide (eDG) which she states is accessible to the public. To date that has not been made available to the public, all areas are flagged as restricted, and we request that it be made accessible to the public as soon as possible.

We want to see institution of a lost records fine, wherein if Social Security loses a claimants records/files an immediate $1000 fine must be paid to the claimant.

Funding

The Commissioner has stated in the past: "Since funding is the fuel that drives our ability to meet the needs of the people who rely on our services, I must tell you that there are very real consequences when we have reduced resources. Under the current performance-based budgets, there is a certain amount of work that can be done for a certain amount of funding, and when our portfolio of traditional work and the new workloads I have described expands without funding, our effectiveness is jeopardized."

We agree with the Commissioner that proper funding is crucial to the success of SSA programs and there are severe, very real consequences to claimants when SSA has reduced resources, yet it is my understanding that she has imposed a hiring reduction. SSA has already experienced staffing cuts in 2006, and based on the President's proposed budget, is expected to experience even more staffing cuts in 2007. The SSA will now have only a 1 of 8 employee replacement ratio for those leaving SSA and who work directly on the front lines in the field offices. This is a claimant's primary interview contact in the disability claims and appeals process, and this staffing cut is a great cause of concern for us. Even now there is not enough staff to handle the current workloads, and the influx of new disability claims is only going to increase over time as the population ages, and we face very turbulent times ahead. The idea that the Commissioner would use these resources she has been given, to create new levels of claims processing, that in reality will make the system tougher on claimants to access benefits, instead of properly staff the program and make it more claimant friendly is a travesty and waste of tax payer dollars. We ask that Congress legislate to ensure that the Social Security trust fund should never be touched for anything else but to pay benefits to the people who are entitled to it, and that the SSA does not have to compete for appropriation funds. We also call on Congress and the GAO to step in, and prevent the Commissioner's very detrimental staffing cut from taking place.

Communication Between SSA And Its Customers Is Crucial/DCM/QDD

Increased contact with claimants throughout WHOLE disability claims process is crucial to the success of the program. Currently there is virtually no communication with claimants after initial intake, written denial, approval, review notices or if by chance the claimant is able to get through to the 1–800 number to ask a question. A welcome step in that direction is the Disability Claims Manager (DCM) pilot where the claimant is able interact on a regular basis in SSA field offices with the person who would be making the decision on their case. If trained properly we believe that DCM staff could perform this role, and it is my understanding that in the pilot these managers processed claims faster and more accurately than the state DDS offices do now. We are very pleased to see the Commissioner's creation of the Quick Disability Determination Unit (QDD) process for the obviously disabled which is long overdue, especially for those who suffer from terminal illness, who currently in many cases, die before they get approved for benefits. We must state that though, that it would better serve its clients if it were part of the SSA field office as well. Also a claimant should be allowed to review all records in their case file at any time, during all phases of the SSDI/SSI process. Currently they are only allowed to review their file after a denial in the initial phase is issued. Before a denial is issued at any stage, the applicant should be contacted as to ALL the sources being used to make the judgment. It must be accompanied by a detailed report as to why a denial might be imminent, who made the determination and a phone number or address where they could be contacted. In case info is missing or they were given inaccurate information the applicant can provide the corrected or missing information before a determination is made. This would eliminate many cases from having to advance to any hearing phase.

Consolidation/Coordination—The Disability Common Sense Approach

The most ideal customer service scenario would be to have ALL phases of the disability claims process be handled directly out of the SSA field offices. Since SSDI/SSI are Federal benefits why has a State DDS level been added to this process at all? We must question why this common sense solution is not being instituted as part of the DSI. We ask that SSA, Congress and the GAO to look into reforming this program in such a way that ALL who handle benefit claims are Federal employees and consolidate ALL phases of the SSDI/SSI process into the individual SSA field offices throughout the nation. More Federal funding is necessary to continue to create a universal network between all outlets that handle SSDI/SSI cases so that claimant's info is easily available to caseworkers handling claims no matter what level/stage they are at in the system. Since eDib is not fully functional at this time, and even when it is, keeping as much of the disability process as possible in the SSA field offices would dramatically cut down on transfer of files and the number of missing file incidences, result in better tracking of claims status, and allow for greater ease in submitting ongoing updated medical evidence in order to prove a claim. In addition, all SSA forms and reports should be made available online for claimants, medical professionals, SSD caseworkers and attorneys, and be uniform throughout the system. One universal form should be used by claimants, doctors, attorneys and SSD caseworkers, which will save time, create ease in tracking status, updating info and reduce duplication of paperwork. Forms should be revised to be more comprehensive for evaluating a claimant's disability and better coordinated with the SS Doctor's Bluebook Listing of Impairments.

5-Month Withholding/Waiting Period For Benefits

Remove 5-month waiting period for SSDI/SSI benefits. Supposedly this law was instituted because it was felt by Congress that the majority of Americans have short and long term disability insurance through their employers. In fact according to the Labor Department's National Compensation Survey released in March 2006, only 40% of U.S. employers offer short-term disability, and only 30% offer long-term disability. We now live in a climate where employer sponsored benefits are in fact decreasing, while as the population ages the need for them is increasing. There is absolutely no good reason for withholding these funds and it is basically robbery of 5 months of their hard earned benefits! Also prime rate bank interest should be paid on all retro payments from first date of filing, due to claimants, as they are losing this as well while waiting for their benefits to be approved. The amount of money withheld during this time could mean the very difference between a more secure future or financial ruin for a population who can no longer work and that will never be able to recoup that loss of back benefits that they are subjected to. It could determine whether or not a person will have to file for State assistance in addition to their Federal benefits and then have to rely on two support programs rather than just one for the rest of their lives. Now more than ever it is time for Congress to remove this additional hindrance to disabled Americans.

Medicare Sligibility/24-Month Waiting Period/Accelerated Benefits Trail/ Mental Health Treatment Study/AI Demonstratrations,

The Commissioner's proposed Accelerated Benefits trial ignored our request to get Congress to legislate removal of 24-month waiting period for ALL Social Security Disability recipients to get full Medicare coverage. That needs to change and we ask this Committee to institute the necessary legislation to remove it as soon as possible. Her suggestion to only allow claimant's whose have medical conditions that are expected to improve within 2–3 years is blatant discrimination against the disabled citizens who need Medicare the most. This proves a total lack of understanding on her part, of how crucial these benefits are to someone who is disabled and can no longer work. Imposing this waiting period, also forces many to have to file for Medicaid/Social Service programs who otherwise may not have needed these services if Medicare was provided immediately upon approval of disability benefits. My organization agrees totally with the Medicare Rights Center, that coverage under all parts of Medicare must start immediately for them, upon disability date of eligibility. As part of the Mental Health Treatment Study and HIV/AI Demonstrations, the Commissioner states that SSA will provide comprehensive health care to DI beneficiaries who have schizophrenia or affective disorders, HIV/AI disorders. Again this should be extended to ALL SSDI claimants regardless of possible work outcome!

Claims Processing Times/Dire Needs/Compensation For Losses Incurred While Waiting For Benefits

We are calling for All SSD case decisions to be determined within three months maximum of original filing date. When it is impossible to do so a maximum of six months will be allowed for appeals, hearings etc—NO EXCEPTIONS. Failure to do so on the part of the SSA will constitute a fine of $500 per week for every week over the six month period—payable to claimants in addition to their awarded benefit payments and due immediately along with their retro pay upon approval of their claim. A dire needs case in the eyes of the SSA means that you have to prove in writing, that you are going to have your home foreclosed on, be evicted from your apartment or have your utilities shut off. Nobody should ever have to deal with that sort of thing when they are sick! Many claimants are also unable to afford health insurance, medicine, food, other necessities of life, and have to wipe out their financial resources because of their inability to work, but even that is not considered a dire need! Worsening health doesn't seem to be much of a factor in speeding up SSD claims either, as there are several reported cases of people who have died while waiting to get their benefits. This is outrageous when something this serious, and a matter of life and death, could be handled in such a poor manner. No other company or other government organization operates with such horrible turn around times. As a result we are calling for Congress to legislate that the SSA will be held financially responsible to reimburse claimants for any loss of property, automobiles, IRA's, pension funds, who incur a compromised credit rating or lose their health insurance as a result of any delay in processing of their claims, which may occur during or after (if there is failure to fully process claim within six months) the initial six month allotted processing period.

Treating Physicians

All doctors should be required by law, before they receive their medical license, and it be made a part of their continuing education program to keep their license, to attend seminars provided free of charge by the SSA, in proper procedures for writing medical reports and filling out forms for Social Security Disability and SSD claimants. Often claimants cannot get their doctors to fill out SSA forms due to time constraints and staffing problems or they have no access to any kind of medical care at all. SSA field offices should also, when a person applies for disability benefits, provide at no charge to the claimant, a listing of free/low cost healthcare resources that they may need to utilize in order prove their disabilities. While the SSA in such cases may order a claimant to go for an IME in these situations, they cannot adequately determine a claimants disability in one visit like a treating physician who see a claimant on a regular basis can.

Proper Weight of Treating Physician Reports/Evidence And IME/Consultative

Too much weight at the initial time of filing, and throughout the claims process is put on the independent medical examiner's and SS caseworker's opinion of a claim. The independent medical examiner, SS caseworker only sees you for a few minutes and has no idea how a patient's medical problems affect their lives after only a brief visit with them. The caseworker at the DDS office never sees a claimant. The decisions should be based with priority given to the claimant's own treating physicians opinions and medical records. When evidence is lacking in that area, and SSD requires a medical exam, it should only be performed by board certified independent doctors who are specialists in the disabling condition that a claimant has (example—Rheumatologists for autoimmune disorders, Psychologists and Psychiatrists for mental disorders). Currently this is often not the case. Also independent medical exams requested by SSA should only be required to be performed by doctors who are located within a 15 mile radius of a claimants residence. If that is not possible—Social Security should provide for transportation or travel expenses incurred for this travel by the claimant.

Easy/Free Acess For Patients To Copies Of Their Own Medical Records

All Americans should be entitled to easy access and FREE copies of their own medical records, including doctor's notes (unless it could be proven that it is detrimental to their health) at all times. This is crucial information for all citizens to have to ensure that they are receiving proper healthcare and a major factor when a person applies for Social Security Disability. Often inaccuracies in these records are never caught, allowing incorrect information to be passed on from doctor to doctor over the years, and could even lead to serious misjudgments in patient care based on bad information.

Removal Of Reconsideration Phase

NY State where I live, is one of the worst in the nation to file a claim for SSDI/SSI benefits, compared to the rest of the nation, especially since 9/11. NY is one of ten test states where the reconsideration phase of the SS Disability claims process was eliminated, causing extraordinary wait times, up to several years in some cases, for claims to be processed At the Buffalo NY DDS office where my own claim for benefits was processed, 48.6% of T2 initial cases, 57.2% of initial cases and 67% of concurrent initial cases were denied. Yet over half of those claims were then approved at the Hearings and Appeals level in the time period between 6/25/05—9/00/05. With initial claims denial rates this high and no opportunity for reconsideration, it only stands to reason that claimants will request a hearing thus forcing them into the court system. Currently in states where the reconsideration phase has been removed there is even a need to ship in ALJ's from other states to help manage the court backlog problem. Yet the SSA Commissioner, has ignored this problem occurring already in these 10 test states and has now passed regulations to remove the reconsideration phase for the whole country, which will continue to force thousands more into the already backlogged Federal Court system. Why waste more Federal dollars on expanding removal of this phase when it has already been proven that it causes even more of a problem to both the claimants and the courts.

Use of Attorneys/ALJ's In Claims Processing

The SSDI/SSI claims process should be set up so there is no need whatsoever for claimant paid legal representation when filing for benefits

Currently the program is set up to line the pockets of the legal system, since a claimant is often encouraged from the minute they apply for benefits to get a lawyer. Why should you need to pay a lawyer to get benefits that you have earned? Every effort should be made to set up the claims process so there is very little need for cases to advance to the hearing and appeal stage since that is where one of the major backlog and wait time exists. It seems that this would create an incentive when work loads at DDS offices are especially high, to rubberstamp denials, moving them to the hearing phase, and pushing their workload into the already overloaded Federal court system, rather than take a little extra time to properly review the claim. The need of lawyers/reps to navigate the system and file claims, and the SSD cap on a lawyer's retro commission is also a disincentive to expeditious claim processing, since purposely delaying the claims process will cause the cap to max out—more money to the lawyer/rep for dragging their feet adding another cost burden to claimants. In other words the system is structured so that it is in a lawyer's best interest for your case to drag on since they get paid 25% of a claimant's retro pay up to $5300—the longer it takes the more they get. From the horror stories I hear from other claimants, many attorneys are definitely taking advantage of that situation. I can't even begin to tell you how many times I am told of people whose health is deteriorating, who are losing their homes and filing for bankruptcy because their attorneys do nothing to try and speed up their claims. Many qualify for dire needs status or are eligible for pre-hearing/review on the record status in order to prevent these problems but are never told that by their attorneys, who sit back and do nothing but collect from a claimant's retro check. Claimants are told that there is a major backlog and since they are unaware of SS regulations they do not question this fraudulent behavior. We view this as a criminal act, yet there is almost oversight on this problem. Instead, from what I have seen in the Commissioner's DSI plan, she is catering to the law community in much the same way that the pharmaceutical companies were catered to when the Medicare Part D plan was instituted. Just as it has with the Medicare program, this adds a greater cost and processing time to the administration of the SSDI program and again adds a financial burden for the disabled. Instead the SSA should provide claimants with a listing in every state, of FREE Social Security Disability advocates/reps when a claim is originally filed in case their services may be needed.

We are not in favor of any changes that would result in more hearings, lesser back payments or a greater reliance on attorneys for claimants to receive benefits. The Commissioner has proposed that a record would be closed after an ALJ issues a decision and new/material evidence would only be allowed to be submitted under certain limited circumstances. This is totally unacceptable, given that a great number of ALJ decisions are currently appealed due to rampant bias against claimants, fraudulent behavior and poor performance by the ALJ's currently serving. We have even heard stories of claimants who are being told by ALJ's that they must give up years of back pay or the judge will not approve their disability claims, which is criminal behavior! We are in favor of audio and/or videotaping of Social Security Disability ALJ hearings and during IME exams allowed at all times to avoid improper conduct by judges and doctors. A copy of court transcript should automatically be provided to claimant or their representative within one month of hearing date FREE of charge. We want to see the institution of a very strict code of conduct for Administrative Law Judges in determining cases and in the courtroom, with fines to be imposed for inappropriate conduct and payable to claimants. We also ask that the GAO review the role of the ALJ in the processing of disability claims and their decision making which has often proven to be very harmful to claimants. We suggest that the GAO and this Subcommittee look at the following report:

General Bias and Administrative Law Judges: Is there a Remedy for Social Security Disability Claimants?

http://organizations.lawschool.cornell.edu/clr/90_3/Vendel_90_Cornell_Law_Review.pdf

Ticket To Work Program—Catch 22—Fear and Mistrust of the SSA

According to SSA disability guidelines: Social Security pays only for total disability. No benefits are payable for partial disability or for short-term disability. You have a valid claim if you have been disabled or are expected to be disabled for 12 consecutive months, or your condition will result in your death. Your condition must interfere with basic work-related activities for your claim to be considered. If your condition is severe but not at the same or equal level of severity as a medical condition on the list, then they must determine if it interferes with your ability to do the work you did previously. If it does not, your claim will be denied. If you cannot do the work you did in the past, SSD looks to see if you are able to adjust to other work. They consider your medical conditions and your age, education, past work experience and any transferable skills you may have. If you cannot adjust to other work, your claim will be approved. If you can adjust to other work, your claim will be denied.

SSA forces the disabled to go through years of abuse trying to prove that they can no longer work ANY job in the national economy due to the severity of their illnesses in order to be approved for benefits. The resulting devastation on their lives, often totally eliminates the possibility of them ever getting well enough to ever return to the workforce, even on a part time basis, in order to utilize the SS Ticket to Work program. Then, sometimes weeks after they are finally approved for SSD/SSI benefits, after their health and finances have been totally destroyed beyond repair, they receive a "Ticket To Work" packet in the mail. A cruel joke to say the least and it is no wonder that the disabled fear continuing disability reviews, utilization of the Ticket to Work Program, and distrust the Federal Government! The Ticket to Work Program is often viewed as a carrot and stick it to the disabled approach.

How Backlogs In The SSDI/SSI Program Place An Increased Burden On The States

Due to the enormous wait times that applicants may endure while waiting for their SSDI/SSI claims to be processed, many are forced into poverty and have to apply for other state funded programs such as Medicaid, food stamps and cash assistance, who wouldn't have needed them, if their disability claims were approved in a timely manner. Another very stressful demeaning process to say the least. This causes an enormous burden across this nation, on those state Social Service programs. This problem would be greatly reduced if the Federal SSD/SSI program was fixed, and the states would definitely reap the benefits in the long run. Also if a healthy person files for Social Service programs and then gets a job, they do not have to reimburse the state once they find a job, for the funds they were given while looking for work. Disability claimants who file for state Social Services assistance while waiting to get SSI benefits in many states, have to pay back the state out of their meager disability benefits once approved, in most cases keeping them below the poverty level and forcing them to continue to use state funded services for the rest of their lives in addition to the Federal SSI program. They are almost never able recover or better themselves, since they can no longer work, and now have to rely on two support programs instead of just one. In all states there should be immediate approval for social services (food stamps, cash assistance, medical assistance, etc.) benefits for SSD claimants that don't have to be paid back to the states out of their SSD benefits once approved. We are calling on the SSA, the GAO and the states to make it a priority to start tracking this connection and act swiftly to correct this problem. Since states are being crushed under the increased Medicaid burden I am sure that this would do a great deal to alleviate that problem as well.

Continuing Disability Reviews

We have heard that there is a proposal to give SSD recipients a limited amount of time to collect their benefits. We are very concerned with the changes that could take place. Since every patient is different and their disabilities are as well, this type of "cookie cutter" approach is out of the question. We especially feel that people with psychological injuries or illness would be a target for this type of action. Some medical plans pay 80% for treatment of biological mental heath conditions, but currently Medicare only pays 50% for an appointment with a psychiatrist. This often prohibits patients from getting proper treatment and comply with rules for continual care on disability. The current disability review process in itself is very detrimental to a patient's health. Many people suffer from chronic conditions that have NO cures and over time these diseases grow progressively worse with no hope of recovery or returning to the workforce. The threat of possible benefits cut off, and stress of a review by Social Security again is very detrimental to a recipients health. This factor needs to be taken into consideration when reforming the CDR process. In those cases total elimination of CDR's should be considered or a longer period of time between reviews such as 10–15 years rather then every 3–7 years, as is currently the case. This would save the SSA a great deal of time, money and paperwork which could then be used to get new claimants through the system faster.

Unless everyone of the concerns/issues outlined above is addressed and resolved in a timely manner, the SSA, Congress and the State governments will continue to fail at what they were put in place to do—serve the people. Most of us were once hard working, tax paying citizens with hopes and "American dreams" but due to an unfortunate accident or illness, have become disabled to a point where we can no longer work. Does that mean we are not valuable to our country, or give the government/society the right to ignore or even abuse us? I think not! We are your mothers, fathers, sisters, brothers, children, friends and acquaintances, and most people think that this could ever happen to them. Remember that at any point in time you too could be facing our dilemma and contrary to what may be popular opinion, nobody willingly chooses this type of existence. I only hope that I can live long enough to see you do what is right for all of us. Since we can no longer work due to our disabilities, we are often considered "disposable" people by general and government standards. In addition our cries and screams are often ignored, many preferring that we just shut up or die. I am here to tell you those days are over now. We are watching, we are waiting, we may be disabled but we vote! Thank you for your time.

Please check out my website at:

http://www.frontiernet.net/~lindafl/bump.html/

Statement of Earl Tucker

My Name is Earl Tucker. I am President of AFGE Council 224 which represents the Quality Assurance workers in the Social Security Administration.

The Social Security Administration's (SSA) is facing major challenges today because of staffing and resource shortages everywhere and not just in processing our disability cases. The "Improved Disability Determination Process" does not cure the lack of necessary resources to do the job. Even with this new process, it is still going to require an additional $1.2 billion over a ten years period to process disability cases. I think this money could be well spent funding the current process and hiring more staffing. More staffing alone would improve the processing of disability cases without spending over a billion dollar on a plan that may or may not improve the process.

Now that the rules have been finalized on the new disability plan, I still have the same questions that I asked on the proposed rules for the disability plan and some questions even prior to the publishing of the proposed rules. On the proposed rules and prior, these were some of the questions that I asked:

Below you will find some specific comments to the 79 pages of the proposal. I will be using printed page numbers for reference.

3rd paragraph under "Program Trends" discusses the increase in DIB claims and the greater complexity of claims (due to more mental claims and vocational related issues) that have caused larger workloads. It is still unclear how the new system will resolve the complexity of these cases. These cases still require a sufficient number of staff with adequate training that have access to reference materials. That's the solution, which can be done under the current system.

5th paragraph of Page 5 states that eDib alone is not enough to improve the system. According to the SSA Commissioner, they have to change the process "to significantly improve disability adjudicators." Again, how is this manifested? A good adjudicator is one that is trained, resourced, experienced and not subject to arbitrary speed-up quotas.

Another thing to keep in mind is that an eDib claim takes longer to review by a DQB examiner than a paper one when you have to screen all the pages on a desktop computer monitor page by page subject to the speed of the program and navigate around the file.

See midway down on page 6 where they discuss "both in-line and end-of-line" QA "at every step of the process." They still have to detail how this will be done. How exactly do you complete an "in-line" review of a disability case? Do you halt case development to critique how one handles a medical source while another is on the way that could resolve some issue?

Go to Paragraph 5 on page 9 that goes into the changes. Again, they boast of a processing time reduced by 25% without providing the basis for this. How can this be done if you replace the Reconsideration second level review with a Reviewing Official step and the Appeals Council with the Decision Review Board while still retaining the initial step and the ALJ? You still have the same number of steps, so where is the reduction in time by these changes.

The need for a Quick Disability Determination unit (completing easy cases in 20 days) seems dubious. We already have provisions to do Presumptive and Teri cases to expedite a decision. People who are "obviously disabled" already receive fast decisions from the DDS, so how will another bureaucratic restructuring solve any problems? Likely reasons for these cases not being allowed ASAP would be mailing issues, securing adequate documentation, inadequate staffing and increasing work loads at the DDS. How will the Quick Unit resolve these issues? NADE wrote that SSA stated that the DDS could not make these allowances "since they wouldn't have access to medical specialties able to make these diagnoses." Why not give them the access? Weren't all components in the process going to have access to the "same medical and/or vocational experts?"

Under "State Agency Determinations" on Page 11, they restate the need to document and explain the basis for every decision. This is one of the most important things at all levels. This will not happen with only a program reshuffle.

Also on Page 11 is a section on "Expertise and the Federal Expert Unit." The concept of a national network of medical and vocational experts is worthy. However, other considerations must be kept in mind. How can an adequate, independent quality review be completed if every component in the system uses the same medical and vocational experts? Often DDS errors are caused by inadequate or incorrect input from their medical or vocational staff. Just how likely would an error from a centralized source be rectified if they are also the quality review source? A resolution may involve different national networks for different components (DDS, ROQA/DQB, OHA).

Under "Reviewing Official" on page 13, they describe the Reconsideration Step as a "rubber stamp" with no "appreciable value." Our experience as a DQB examiners does not bear this out. Reconsiderations many times do reverse initial decisions and they are regularly sampled by the DQB. Moreover, a current successful program has New York DDS reviewing the Recons of New Jersey and Maryland DDS'. Such a system would preclude even the appearance of a "rubber stamp" in addition to having a truly independent second pair of eyes from a different DDS reviewing the claim.

I also find it silly to mandate that these Reviewing Officials have to be attorneys. On the penultimate paragraph on Page 13, they list the reasons (or delusions really) why attorneys should do this. Yet, the Commissioner forgets that ALJs are attorneys and that studies have found that they often make mistakes. Law schools do not train you for Social Security disability sequential evaluation process. The ability to adjudicate and explicate as directed by policy are the important skills. They are inculcated and maintained with experience, adequate training, and resource access whether you go to law school or not. Moreover, it is unclear if an adequate number of attorneys could be attracted at the current salary levels offered.

Also, please note in the second paragraph of page 14 that the Reviewing Official (even though he is a lawyer!) still has to send the claim to the Federal Expert Unit (and delay adjudication) before denying the claim again. When workloads increase, employees may feel pressure to allow the claims to avoid "timeliness" delays.

An important section for us is "Ensuring Quality" on page 23. They again fawn on "in-line" review of cases without detailing how to do this. Most importantly, the Commissioner pushes the replacement of DQB's with a "new centrally-managed quality assurance system," but she fails to detail or explain how this will be done. How more "centrally managed" could an organization be that reviewed over 326,000 cases in FY 2004? Currently, 10 regional offices answer to a central office whose job is to maintain consistency. Even with eDib, there will be some variance how different people, units, or offices view a case. Moreover, how will more centralization "encourage local flexibility?" Another issue is how a totally centralized office could handle all the local court-case mandates and idiosyncrasies of case development nationwide.

See the second paragraph on page 24 about judging "service, timeliness, productivity, and cost as components of quality along with accuracy." I addressed this abstract and untenable wish in my Lewin Report review.

Please See page 29 concerning Reopening. This extreme restriction of its application is a bad idea. It is not uncommon that DQB examiners reopen prior claims under the current rules. In this way we can correct prior denials so that do not have to go through the OHA process. A common scenario involves people with mental illness who cannot follow deadlines due to their condition. The restriction on reopening will be a disservice to some of the most vulnerable people in society and propel cases to the OHA that can be resolved beforehand.

Page 31 lists the costs for the proposed rules which are 1.2 billion dollars between 2006 and 2015, according to the Office of the Chief Actuary. Considering how such estimates usually understate costs and that there are often unforeseen, unfunded hurdles, will long-standing budget deficits permit such expenses? As always, a proper system needs proper funding. Our current system has been cheated for a while, so why should we think that the new system will be funded as it should?

These are some additional Questions that I had long before the proposed disability plan:

1) The GAO recently found that the cost-benefit analysis of SSA had underestimated the costs of eDib. What are your current cost projections for eDib and how

much do you expect it to save SSA and the Trust fund? What are these figures based on?

2) In your testimony before the House Ways and Means Committee, you stated that "a shift to inline quality review would provide greater opportunities for identifying problem areas and implementing corrective actions and related training." Moreover, "an in-line quality review process managed by the DDSs and a centralized quality control unit would replace the current SSA quality control system." Later, NADE reported in their meeting with you on 10/24/03 that SSA agreed with having PER reviews "done centrally" and "that DQB will not exist, as we know it."

What are your exact plans for the DQB staff and why are you doing this considering the time and effort spent on the proposition that the PER review expanded to Title XVI for greater DQB review? Why do you want to replace a disability quality assurance system that saves the American taxpayer more than $13 for very $1 invested and has saved over $300 million annually for the Trust funds? Prior to the PER review, SSA operations and state DDS' reviewed their own work resulting in a program in disarray and requiring Congress to mandate an independent PER review. Why do we want to risk this again? How will accuracy be increased in this system? How likely is it that Congress will alter the statutory requirements of PER?

3) What has been the impact and influence of the November 2000 report of the Lewin Group and the Pugh, Ettinger, McCarthy Associates upon your proposed disability program? Were they consulted or did they have any input on the new system? When will Booz, Allen, Hamilton finish their review of the California DDS inline quality review and will their report be made available to us?

4) Can the new disability system function without your requested increases in the Service Delivery Budget? Couldn't an increased budget be used to adequately fund the current system? The major criticisms you mentioned about the current approach involve inadequate documentation and waiting times. These problems are caused by staffing issues and work load demands, which with proper budgeting could be minimized in the process currently.

5) Why is an Expert Review (ER) panel needed for Quick Decisions if we have a presumptive allowance process for SSI cases that can be used by the FO and the DDS to currently allow these cases expeditiously? People who are "obviously disabled" already receive fast decisions from the DDS, so how will another bureaucratic grouping solve scenarios that do not currently exist? Likely reasons for these cases not being allowed ASAP would be mailing issues, documentation securing, and inadequate staffing and increasing work loads at the DDS. How will the ER resolve these issues? NADE wrote that SSA stated how the DDS could not make these allowances "since they wouldn't have access to medical specialties able to make these diagnoses." Why not give them the access? Weren't all components in the process going to have access to the "same medical and/or vocational experts?" Moreover, who is going to provide independent quality review of the ER panel?

6) How can an adequate, independent quality review be completed if every component in the system uses the same medical and vocational experts? Often DDS errors are caused by inadequate or incorrect input from their medical or vocational staff. Just how likely would an error from a centralized source be rectified if they are also the quality review source?

7) How will no SSA employee be "adversely affected" by your approach if the quality review is centralized, DQBs are "eliminated," and eDib greatly reduces the current work of Program Assistants?

8) On what basis do you assert that "processing time will be reduced by at least 25%" if you add an ER and replace the reconsideration step with a Reviewing Official (besides the demands required by reviewing the pilot projects that may become national)?

9) Our Regional Director has been telling us that the new approach would only effect the QA review in order to mollify us, but this seem very unlikely. The new approach would totally change how the PER and QA process is completed. How could this be done without DQBs since PER review is mandated by Congress?

10) With the current DQB organizational structure, the performance of any DDS can be scientifically validated. How do you plan to validate statistically the performance of each DDS without the DQBs? Do you want to know the actual performance of each DDS? Do you only want a statistically valid DDS' performance at the national level?

11) There are many Acquiescence Rulings by the United States District Courts that differ from one District Court to another. How will Acquiescence Rulings of the different District Courts be handle centrally?

In conclusion, the current process has always been under funded and cheated since day one. I believe it still would work if properly funded. I don't see Congress spending an additional $1.2 billions over 10 years to implement this new disability plan.

Earl Tucker

Statement of C. Richard Dann, Union of American Physicians and Dentists

We are submitting this statement for the record for the June 15, 2006 Hearing on Social Security Disability Service Improvement on behalf of the Union of Physicians and Dentists (UAPD)/American Federation of State, County and Municipal Employees (AFSCME), AFL–CIO. UAPD represents 140 Medical Consultants in California's Disability Determination Services (DDS) and AFSCME represents 1.4 million public service and health care workers.

UAPD has been monitoring proposed changes to the Social Security Disability process since the Redesign was first proposed in April 1994. We have offered written comments to the Social Security Administration (SSA) and our members have testified before this Subcommittee in the past with suggestions to improve the Disability process.

With final regulations in place, our members stand ready to implement the new system. And, while we agree that many of the changes will improve the system, we have grave concerns about one requirement that is yet to be determined—specifically the qualifications for the position of Medical Expert in the Medical and Vocational Expert System (MVES). The final regulations indicated that the Social Security Commissioner will publish the requirements for these positions at a later date. Therefore, our comments will focus on the requirements that are under consideration by the Commissioner.

Last year the Institute of Medicine issued an interim report on the qualifications and organization of Medical Consultants in the New Disability Process. The Institute report recommended that all Medical Consultants and Medical Examiners at the state and federal levels be Board certified. We strongly disagree and are concerned that the Commissioner will rely upon this flawed analysis to implement these recommendations in her final guidelines. Board certification requirements will not enhance the speed or accuracy of adjudication, would greatly limit the number of potential candidates, creating a large backlog in the DDDs, and is simply not practical.

Commissioner Barnhart has expressed concerns that various medical specialties are not readily available to all DDS adjudicators. However, there is a very limited need for such specialty consultation; well-versed generalists who understand the processes, treatments and prognosis for a wide range of diseases, as well as the federal statutes, are better qualified than specialists to make the vast majority of disability assessments at the state DDSs.

The standard medical model in the United States and most countries is that generalist providers initially evaluate patients so only the most ill or complicated cases are referred to specialists, effectively utilizing their unique skills. The factors to determine functional impairment are relatively simple and succinct: the ability to lift, carry, stand, walk, sit, reach, grasp, turn, push, pull, pinch, feel, bend, squat, climb, crawl, reach, see, hear, speak, and environmental tolerances do not require specialty assessment. The basic findings for gait, station, range of motion, strength, dexterity, sensation, balance, vision and hearing are fairly simple medical concepts, and understanding of those factors is not enhanced significantly by specialty training.

A specialist's capabilities are not needed on every case involving that specialty. For example, although hypertension involves the cardiovascular system, the vast majority of blood pressure prescribing is done by generalists, not cardiologists. The vast majority of care for back pain is similarly done by generalist MDs, not orthopedists. Specialists are rarely better equipped to adjudicate most SSA Disability cases than generalists.

We strongly oppose replacing Medical Consultants with non-physician providers in DDS or MVES. While arbitrarily urging Board certification of all physicians and PhDs in the Program, the Commissioner has paradoxically indicated that they already are recruiting for nurse consultants for the Boston rollout of the new process. Use of these other less credentialed medical sources offers no advantages; they have less medical training and knowledge than the physicians and PhDs employed currently as Medical Consultants, with the disadvantage of decreased legal defensibility in appeals.

The DDS and Regional offices rely heavily Medical Consultants and it is estimated that currently five percent or less of the system's PhD Medical Consultants are Board certified. Requiring Board certification would leave a gaping hole in Psychiatric Medical Consultant capability, an area currently underserved in some states. Affordability and availability are the major obstacles to increasing the numbers of medical specialist experts in the SSA Disability program. The Institute report further recommended a grandfather period of five years for current non-Board certified Medical Consultants. After that period, those Medical Consultants without Board certification are presumed suddenly not to be qualified to make the same assessments that they have been making for five, ten or fifteen years.

Most current Medical Consultants are mid to late career professionals, and Board certification was not as prevalent 25 years ago. Board certification requires multiple years of in-hospital residency training and passing Board examinations, and is just not feasible for a mid or late career DDS Medical Consultants. If SSA makes Board certification mandatory, it should apply to new applicants only, and incumbent MCs should be grandfathered. Any less accommodating policy will result in acute MC shortages and increased costs due to the higher salaries board certified doctors would demand.

And, finally, requiring Board certification is impractical because most National Medical Boards require Recertification after five or ten years. Most recertification's require ongoing practice in that specialty area since last certification, as well as passage of a written examination. If SSA imposes this requirement, many medical consultants would not qualify for Board recertification because they would not have been in practice in their specialty.

As an alternative, we strongly endorse federal standardization of Medical Consultant training and would like to emphasize that this is not a new idea. After over ten years of work by a group of DDS Training Coordinators, DDS Medical Consultants, Central Office Training staff, and Central Office Medical Consultants, a national SSA Disability Medical Consultant Training Curriculum was finally completed. A UAPD medical consultant was one of the members of that SSA workgroup.

We also would like to point out that the Board certification will not solve the problem of the high reversal rate by the Administrative Law Judges (ALJs). The reasons for this discrepancy in the decision making process between the ALJs and the DDSs are actually pretty simple: the ALJ receives minimal medical training (typically two weeks in California, the nation's largest DDS) and there is currently no SSA quality review of ALJ decisions as there is for DDS decisions. The ALJ makes decisions based on "substantial evidence," rather than the "preponderance of evidence" standard that the DDS applies. Our members who review cases for Continuing Disability Review (CDR) might find the following scenario: two DDS teams (initial and reconsideration) considered all evidence and arrived at a decision of "no severe or minimal impairment;" an ALJ then heard the case and, based on poorly substantiated endorsement of disability from a treating source, assessed the claimant "disabled." This likely allowance error cannot be reversed at the next CDR due to the "Medical Improvement Review Standard." Under this standard, the primary assessment on a CDR is not current assessment of disability, but rather an assessment of whether "significant medical improvement" has occurred since the last assessment of disability. If the two DDS teams judged that the claimant was capable of extensive work but the ALJ ruled that they were extremely limited with the same findings, subsequent CDRs will virtually never be able to show "significant medical improvement." That seems quite contrary to the Commissioners goal of "fostering a return to work at all stages."

The need for consistency between DDS and ALJ decisions is a very old problem. Many attempts have been made to resolve it. In the 1990s Process Unification Training was undertaken to increase the rate of DDS allowances and decrease the number of ALJ reversals. DDS allowances increased, but ALJ allowance rates have not fallen appreciably. ALJ decisions should use the same standards as the DDS, should be subject to quality review, should have the same accountability, and a mechanism to reverse ALJ decisions unsupported by the evidence on CDRs.

We appreciate the opportunity to offer our perspective to this Subcommittee and we also urge the Subcommittee members to ensure that there are adequate resources for the current process and for implementation of the new process. There already ar
cient fund
ity service